Contents

Figures

Tables

Contributors

Craig Anderson is a chartered surveyor who completed his Doctorate in Organisational and Environmental Psychology, majoring in Organisational Learning. He has held teaching/research appointments at the University of Strathclyde, Strathclyde Graduate School of Business, the College of Estate Management and the National University of Singapore. His consultancy and research interests are in the fields of workplace strategy, organisational communications, diagnosis and learning, and on the use of creativity in ideas generation and problem solving. He was formally Director of Strategic Planning with a global media, PR and advertising Service Group based in the Asia pacific region. He currently works as a management consultant specialising in workplace strategy and is a tutor at Strathclyde Graduate School of Business.

Ghassan Aouad is Professor of Construction Information Technology at the School of Construction and Property Management of the Faculty of Business and Informatics of the University of Salford. He is currently the Associate Head of School Research and has written extensively about IT and construction. He is visiting Professor in ESAI, Portugal, and is regularly invited to participate in conferences worldwide.

Pauline Ärlebäck holds a Master degree in Business Administration and a Bachelor degree in Economics. She is currently working as a project manager of marketing events in a smaller Swedish hi-tech firm. Together with professor Rapp she has written a report on the use of videoconferences in a number of large Swedish companies.

Nic Beech is Director of Academic Matters and Senior Lecturer in Human Resource Management at Strathclyde Graduate School of Business. He has an academic background in sociology and philosophy, and his work experience and subsequent doctoral studies were in HRM. His research interests are in interactional and trans-disciplinary study of management. He is co-author of *The Essence of HRM* (Prentice Hall, 1995).

George Cairns is a Senior Lecturer in management at Strathclyde Graduate School of Business. He researches on the relationship between the physical and social environments of organisations, and the inputs of users to organisational change processes.

Cristina Caramelo Gomes is Professor of IT and Ergonomics at the Architecture Faculty of Universidade Lusiada, Portugal. She has a PhD in Business and Informatics from the University of Salford and has written widely in the area of the new methods of work and ergonomics, architectural design and facilities management, and has presented papers at conferences across Europe. Her present research interests focus on the sustainability of new methods of work.

Lisa Harris is a Lecturer in the School of Business and Management at Brunel University and Course Director of the eCommerce BSc. She holds an MBA, a PhD in Technology Management and is a Chartered Marketer. She teaches Marketing and eCommerce courses for both the University and the Chartered Institute of Marketing, and is the Secretary of the CIM's Royal Counties Branch. Her research interests are currently focused upon the management challenges faced by traditional organisations that are seeking to introduce eCommerce strategies.

Paul Jackson is Lecturer in Management Studies at Brunel University. He has a PhD in Management Studies from the University of Cambridge and has been a European Union Research Fellow at the Work and Organization Research Centre at Tilburg University, the Netherlands. He has written widely in the area of information technology and new methods of work, and is currently undertaking researching on organisational change and eBusiness, eGovernment and organisational networking. He has edited two previous books with Routledge: *Virtual Working: Social and Organisational Dynamics* and *Teleworking: International Perspectives* (with Jos van der Wielen).

Pertti Järvinen is Professor of Information Systems and Computing Milieus at the University of Tampere, Finland. His research interests are in research methods, social effects of computing systems, information systems development and managing the information function. He is an associate editor of *The Information Society*. He has published a book *On Research Methods*, and articles in journals such as *Information and Management*, *Operations Research* and *AI + Society*. He has been using the special reviewing approach in his doctoral seminar for more than 10 years (see http://www.uta.fi/~pj/)

Gerry Kincaid is the Information Systems Director with the Datum Group. His background is in computing science and economics, and in addition to holding an MBA he is a professional engineer. Gerry was part of the MBO team which took a British Shipbuilders' subsidiary into the private sector and has developed systems in use in eCommerce providers and primary healthcare systems in use in over one hundred general practices.

Diana Limburg is an Assistant Professor in the faculty of Management Studies at Twente University, The Netherlands. She is in the final stages of her PhD on introducing telework. Her research interests lie in the area of the management of IT-related change, user-participation and the impact of IT on the work organisation.

Martin van der Linden undertook an undergraduate course of Interior, Furniture and Product Design at the Academie voor Beeldende Kunsten in Maastricht, the Netherlands, and also studied at Tokyo University in 1992. He worked for Hiroshi Hara in Tokyo on the Umeda Interconnected tower and the new Kyoto station. He received a 2-year scholarship and did postgraduate studies at the Southbank University in London, which included an MSc in Engineering Product Design and Postgraduate Diploma in Architecture. He has participated in various architectural and urban competitions and established van der Architects in 1995 in London, a design consultancy firm. Clients include Nokia, Celestica and Microsoft. Since 1999 he has been a lecturer and researcher at Waseda University in Tokyo.

James McCalman is Reader in Organisational Behaviour and Head of Brunel University's Graduate Business School. A senior management academic with business experience and a research and publishing record, he has wide experience of teaching, research and consulting in the UK, Europe, Southeast Asia and the United States. Dr. McCalman was formerly Director of Education and Training for a major US healthcare firm and consults widely on organisational change issues and the introduction of self-managed teams. Dr McCalman is the author of six books, eight book chapters and numerous academic and management journal articles.

Marcus Ormerod, ARICS, is Lecturer at the School of Construction and Property Management of the Faculty of Business and Informatics of the University of Salford. He is Director of Postgraduate Research and Associate Director of the Graduate School. His present research interests are accessible environments, disability issues, aesthetics, education and learning, and visualisation.

Birger Rapp has a chair in Economic Information Systems, Department of Computer and Information Science, Linköping University. He is the head of the department of ISM (Information and System Management) and a board member of the Department of Computer and Information Science. He is the President of the board of the Swedish Teleworking Association, 'Distansforum', and Program Director in Management and Economic Information Systems at IMIT (Institute of Management of Innovation and Technology) and board member of the Archipelago Office. He was an Expert for the 'Distansarbetsutredningen' (The Swedish Public Investigation of Teleworking). Professor Rapp is also the leader of the research-group ITOS (Information Technology and Organisational Structure). He has recently written 'Flexibla organisationslösningar. Om flexibla arbetsformer och flexibla kontor' (Flexible organisational solutions. About flexible forms of work and flexible offices. In Swedish). He has also published books in investment theory, in production planning and in control and teleworking and principal agent theory and a great many papers in international journals. (See also www.ida.liu.se/labs/eis/people/birra.html)

Wendy Spinks is Associate Professor in the Department of Management Science in the Faculty of Engineering Science, University of Tokyo. She was a founding member of the International Flexwork Forum and has served on several telework-related government committees in Japan. Her major research interest is corporate applications of telework. In 1999 she was chair of the organising committee that ran the Fourth ITF International Workshop and business conference that took place in Tokyo.

Reima Suomi has been a Professor of Information Systems Science at Turku School of Economics and Business Administration, Finland since 1994, and is a docent for the universities of Turku and Oulu. He concentrates on topics around management of telecommunications, including issues such as management of networks, electronic and mobile commerce, virtual organisations, telework and competitive advantage through telecommunication-based information systems. His current research interests focus on the tourism industry and healthcare industry. Altogether, Reima has over 200 publications, and has published in journals such as *Information and Management*, *Information Services and Use*, *Technology Analysis and Strategic Management*, *The Journal of Strategic Information Systems* and *Behaviour and Information Technology*.

Guest foreword

Over half of the European workforce now uses a computer at work, mainly for document and information management, and for business communications. Yet, despite this enormous change in workplace technologies, we have yet to see a commensurate change in work organisation or in workplace design: in 2000, only about 6 per cent of the European workforce yet benefits from flexibility in the time and place of work through telework agreements, and heating and lighting of offices, and travel to and between them, is now the largest single resource-use burden on our environment.

Work organisation and workplace redesign are inextricably linked in the evolution towards new sustainable models of economic growth in a knowledge economy. The quality of working-life and the life-work balance that can now be achieved is essential to the higher levels of participation in knowledge work that must be extended into all communities.

This publication is an excellent contribution to further research, and a catalyst for change.

Peter D. Johnston
Head, New Methods of Work
DG-Information Society
European Commission

Preface

The original idea for this book dates back to the international workshop *Tele-working Environments*, hosted in Turku, Finland in the summer of 1998. The workshop discussed the importance of new work developments, such as tele-working, mobile working and other forms of 'virtual work', to a range of organisational and policy agendas. Many papers presented illustrated how new forms of work flexibility challenged the way corporate strategies and policies were conventionally formulated. As such, they highlighted the fact that new intellectual frameworks were needed to help recast approaches to the design of work, and even the design of workplaces themselves.

While the present volume certainly carries forward this debate, it also seeks to locate the issues in the broader contexts within which work is being recon-figured. Perhaps the most important issue here has been the development of *eCommerce*, together with its associated (e)Business models and organisa-tional structures. Such developments have co-evolved with an increase in information and communications technology (ICT)-mediated working, with ICT devices providing the means for the articulation of new organisational forms, as well as for new types of business-to-customer interaction. As a con-sequence, we have seen the development of new types of networked organisa-tion and new forms of virtual collaboration. In addition to this, the growth of so-called 'mCommerce'—the use of mobile telephony in both business and consumer arenas—has given fresh impetus to such notions as mobile working, alternative-officing and knowledge networking.

The key theme running through the book is that while developments in ICTs and business processes call for new ways of designing work and workplaces (not least to take advantage of new forms of spatial flexibility), the context for this is very much set by developments in eBusiness structures, and the new forms of inter- and intra-organisational relationships they engender. The book therefore seeks to forge connections between related issues and phenomena (such as eBusiness networks and their associated working practices), and provide frameworks to help navigate this new landscape. Emphasis is placed on matters of analysis and design, in particular how the design of work and use of space can be planned for and managed in more systemic and effective ways. In so doing, the book seeks to show how organisations can embrace new technologies and business opportunities by creating productive, dynamic and sustainable workplaces that exploit the potential offered by contemporary forms of work flexibility.

One consequence of the above is that the intended audience for the book reaches across disciplinary and professional boundaries. It shows how architects and facilities managers need to be conversant with the changing nature of work, particularly the emerging forms of spatial flexibility. For eBusiness strategists, there are important lessons in terms of the job design implications of new business structures and processes. The book will also have much to say to students of eCommerce, information systems design, and the management of innovation and organisational change. But wherever you are standing now, we hope you can use this book as a way of looking beyond conventional boundaries and find new ways of tackling issues that lie at the heart of today's organisational developments.

If you would like to get in touch about any ideas contained in this book, please contact paul@pauljackson.org or reima.suomi@tukkk.fi.

Acknowledgements

In putting this book together we are deeply grateful to a number of people who have taken part in, or made possible, the discussions that led to the present volume. Although too many to mention by name, we would particularly like to thank all those who have contributed to the ITF International workshops, especially the events in Finland and Japan. The research presented and the debates that ensued have helped lay the groundwork for many of the ideas below. We would also like to thank the sponsors of these events.

With respect to the 1998 workshop in Turku, Finland, particular thanks go to John Nolan and Peter Johnston of the European Commission DG XIII, who gave the workshop the needed visibility and credibility. Special thanks go to Mats Aspnäs and Laura Hollmén, who had a crucial role in processing the first round of the papers for the original proceedings. Without the support from the workshop programme committee chair, Tapio Reponen, the quality of the papers would not have been as good as it was. Last, but not least, the daily operational work performed by Mrs Birgit Haanmäki to make the workshop a success should also be acknowledged

For the present book, other thanks go to Mal Pate for his hard work and attention to detail in getting the manuscript in a publishable form; and to Catriona King from Routledge for her support and great patience.

1 Introduction

eBusiness issues and workplace design

Paul Jackson

British Prime Minister Winston Churchill once remarked: 'We shape our buildings and thereafter they shape us.' It is an aphorism that workplace designers have been slow to heed. However, as managers, architects and others wake up to the contribution office design makes to an effective work environment, they are also presented with a host of new possibilities in the way work is organised. The key development has been the use of advanced information technologies (IT)—particularly those based around the Internet— to support innovations in business processes and customer services. Added to this has been a growth in corporate call centres, as well as mobile communications (which themselves are increasingly 'Web-enabled'). The result has been a rise in new forms of organisational collaboration, combined with greater spatial flexibility in work and customer interactions.

As discussions of 'eBusiness' demonstrate, there is more to these developments than just IT (see, for example, Tapscott *et al.* 2000; Kalakota and Robinson 2000). Appropriate organisational structures are essential if the new business concepts built upon the technology are to flourish. But this brings its own challenges, not least the need to adapt organisational cultures and ways of working. While the present volume seeks to bring these issues together, it also argues that a further set of problematics be drawn into the frame: the design and use of the workplace.

Debates elsewhere, most notably on 'telework', have long called for a more systemic treatment of IT-enabled change, particularly the need to build bridges with architecture and facilities management (for instance, Jackson and van der Wielen 1998; Robertson 1999). This is not simply because changes brought about by remote and mobile working tend to reduce, as well as modify, the demands made on office environments; it also reflects the importance of good workplace design to organisational effectiveness.

The key issue here is captured by Becker and Steele's (1995) notion of organisational 'ecology'—the idea that the dynamics of a workplace are strongly influenced by the way it is designed and managed:

> (Workplace) size, shape, layout, furnishings, and equipment shape our work lives, at the same time our behaviours, attitudes, and values shape the nature of that designed environment, how it is used and the meanings we attach to it. The ecology of the organisation is an often invisible but nonetheless strong force shaping how people work with each other and how well the organisation performs, especially when conditions demand flexibility and quick responses to new demands.
>
> (Becker and Steele 1995: X)

Concerted attention to these issues has been frustrated by a typical fragmentation in decision-making on workplace design. This concerns a lack of dialogue not only between users and expert groups, but also between experts themselves (e.g. architects, interior designers, information systems planners). As Leaman and Borden point out, the under-performance that results can be explained by the way workers' behaviour and degrees of freedom are 'systematically reduced by decisions over which they themselves have no control' (Leaman and Borden 1993: 16). A more participative approach to design is common in areas such as information system development. However, the present volume is concerned with the broader set of stakeholders that influence the design and use of workplaces.

Such an approach has been advocated by writers such as Becker and Steele (1995), Duffy (1997), Robertson (1999) and Horgen *et al.* (1999). All share the view that a greater integration of stakeholder perspectives and expertise is needed if workplaces are to support the needs and preferences of users, while also improving business performance and making better use of resources. The present volume raises these issues in the context of emerging eBusiness practices. It recognises that in embracing Internet technologies, considerable re-engineering, and even network redesign, may be needed (Tapscott *et al.* 2000, Chapter 2 in this volume by MacCalman and Anderson). This in turn may demand new working methods and business relationships (such as cross-functional teams and enterprise alliances).

The nature of eBusiness changes also presents managers with new location options. In addition, much of the work done may be carried out beyond conventional office settings, as employees operate in nomadic and teleworking modes. Team collaborations may take place 'virtually'—IT being used to support interaction across organisational and spatial boundaries. Competitive pressures and shortage of space may also mean renewed efforts to minimise expenditure on office buildings and facilities while simultaneously enhancing their effectiveness and creativity.

This is a tall challenge. The scale and speed of change is difficult enough without the added complexity of a thoroughgoing treatment of workplace redesign issues. Without such an approach, however, organisations may simply be storing up new problems as they resolve old ones. If nothing else, they will fail to maximise the technological, architectural and human resources available to them. Such an approach challenges professional boundaries. It calls for theoretically informed architects, able to anticipate business developments and changes in the nature of work. It demands a fusion of facilities management and IT support to allow for more rounded responses to employees' needs, providing them with connectivity and workstation space wherever and whenever they choose to work.

The challenge of work redesign in the eBusiness era is well set out by Francis Duffy, former President of the Royal Institute of British Architects, in his account of the 'New Office':

> Managing change must involve simultaneously rethinking the use of human resources, reinventing the ways in which information technology should be used, and redesigning the work environment. And it must be recognised that the ways in which office buildings are procured and managed are as important in determining the quality of the working environment as the physical structures and their interiors.
>
> (Duffy 1997: 10)

The chapters that follow provide insights into the dimensions and points of contact on this topic. The chapters are split into four main parts. In Part 1 of the book, 'eBusiness structures and processes', chapters by James McCalman and Craig Anderson, and by Lisa Harris, address the demands made by eBusiness for new forms of intra and inter-organisational collaboration, and for a redesign of office space and information support. Part 2, 'Workplace architecture and design', with chapters by Cristina Caramelo Gomes, Ghassan Aouad and Marcus Ormerod, and by Martin van der Linden, examines the need for rethinking architectural approaches to building design, particularly the importance of linking the design and management of buildings to the imperatives of IT-supported organisational change and the requirement for more socially and ecologically sustainable ways of working.

In Part 3, 'The design and introduction of new methods of work', frameworks are presented which illustrate the need for more systematic and culturally sensitive approaches to the introduction of new methods of work. Chapters are presented here by Diana Limburg and Wendy Spinks respectively. Finally, Part 4 of the book, 'Rethinking knowledge networking and virtual collaboration', looks at issues raised by collaboration and learning tools intended to improve interaction and knowledge management across social and physical borders. The chapters in question, by Nic Beech, George Cairns and Gerry Kincaid; Birger Rapp and Pauline Ärlebäck; and by Pertii Järvinen, point to a number of key conceptual and methodologies issues that must be broached if we are to understand and manage the new types of work involved.

We hope and believe that the ideas presented in these chapters will lead to more rounded and systematic approaches to today's challenges in workplace redesign. The insights they provide are important not only for producing buildings and systems of work that support and enhance (rather than constrain and frustrate) the actions and options of users. They also lay down a new and integrated agenda for managers and workplace designers as they face up to the world of eBusiness change.

References

Becker, F. and Steele, F. (1995) *Workplace by Design*, San Francisco: Jossey-Bass.

Duffy, F. (1997) *The New Office*, London: Conran Octopus.

Horgen, T.H., Joroff, M.L., Porter, W.L. and Schön, D.A. (1999) *Excellence by Design: transforming workplace and work practice*, New York: John Wiley.

Jackson, P.J. and van der Wielen, J.M. (eds) (1998) *Teleworking. International Perspectives: from telecommuting to the virtual organisation*, London: Routledge.

Kalakota, R. and Robinson, M. (2000) *e-Business 2.0: roadmap for success*, Harlow: Addison Wesley.

Leaman, A. and Borden, I. (1993) 'The responsible workplace: user expectations', in Duffy, F., Crisp, V.H.C. and Laing, A. (eds) *The Responsible Workplace: the redesign of work and offices*, Oxford: Butterworth Architecture in association with Estates Gazette.

Robertson, K. (1999) *Work Transformation: planning and implementing the new workplace*, New York: HNB Publishing.

Tapscott, D., Ticoll, D. and Lowy, A. (2000) *Digital Capital: harnessing the power of business webs*, London: Nicolas Brealy.

Part 1

eBusiness structures and processes

In Part 1 we are concerned with the way developments in eBusiness and the Internet are affecting organisational structures and processes. Chapter 2 by James McCalman and Craig Anderson examines how workplace design can be used to provide a better integration of the physical work environment with IT and flexible working. The management of eBusiness, they argue, must analyse the impact between organisational structures, teamwork and intra and inter-firm collaboration. Central to this is the concept of 'corporate nomads'—flexible workers who mingle their use of workspace and time with supporting technology in order to undertake work tasks, and liaise with clients and team members.

McCalman and Anderson note that many businesses engaged in eBusiness change are looking to IT as a way of supporting the redesign of office space, particularly in terms of minimising the fixed costs of occupancy. In so doing, they say, businesses must confront the need to accommodate fluctuations in the number and locations of personnel brought about by the turbulence in market conditions. The authors argue that in response to such factors, management is increasingly predisposed towards greater autonomy in work design, which may also involve producing 'smarter working' arrangements by embracing a creative fusion of work environments, technologies and people.

McCalman and Anderson point out that developments in eBusiness have led to a redefinition of the relationships between buyers and suppliers, as well as between businesses and their customers, thereby blurring the boundaries between different parts of the value chain. One consequence of this is a need for business network redesign, encompassing inter-organisational collaboration and greater cross-functional team working. Such developments, they point out, have major consequences for the way work processes and interactions should be supported, both in technological and spatial terms.

The authors remind us that the design of the working environment has long been treated as a marginal and technical matter, premised on a set of values and beliefs that reflect the industrial origins of the workplace. They show, however, how attempts have been made to overcome the constraints in such designs by development of 'intelligent buildings', that is, workplaces with technologies and environments more supportive to human needs and able to respond to change over time. Greater building intelligence, say McCalman and Anderson, is central to creating workplaces that allow individuals and teams to generate, manipulate and distribute knowledge—an essential ingredient in working practices and business relationships in eBusiness design.

The authors substantiate their arguments with an international case study. They conclude that technology alone cannot provide eBusiness with solutions to its problems, particularly given the need for more concerted attention to knowledge creation and management. A much wider approach is needed, which supports the work of individuals and teams at the various spaces and times they may be working. Settings that support informal and formal collaboration, brainstorming and creativity, but also reflection and concentration, will be demanded. This requires, they argue, a thorough understanding of the new ways that organisations function in the eBusiness era, and the central importance of knowledge processes to them.

As with the previous authors, in Chapter 3 Lisa Harris looks at the way eBusiness developments challenge traditional organisational structures, but in this case with particular reference to the issues raised for established marketing practices. The growth of networked and virtual forms of organisation calls for new ways of managing marketing information and interfacing with customers. Indeed, Internet developments, she argues, have heightened the need for new, more agile forms of networking that allow for greater attention to customer value.

Harris highlights, for instance, the emergence of 'meta-mediaries'—Internet-based enterprises that help customers navigate the growing complexity and volume of the Web. For organisations themselves, new communications challenges must also be faced, such as ensuring consistent forms of customer interaction, even where several enterprises within a network are involved. As such, the integration of customer and marketing data becomes essential for the success of new eBusiness structures. In this context Harris also discusses the issues raised by 'clicks and mortar' businesses, especially the matter of 'channel cannibalisation'. She describes how some companies have designed operations around a combination of 'offline' (physical, e.g. high street stores) and 'online' (virtual, e.g. Internet) ways of interacting with customers.

One consequence of these developments is that marketing operations will increasingly need to be based around customer groups, rather than geography or products. This will not only require changes to organisational structures, Harris argues, but new forms of data integration and support that enable better customer profiling, and personalisation of services and offerings, and that generally improve the quality and management of customer relationships.

2 Designing oases for corporate nomads

The impact of facilities management on work design and the flexible workforce

James McCalman and
Craig Anderson

Introduction

Does eBusiness mark the beginning of a revolution? Tapscott (1995) describes its growth as part of the burgeoning of a digital economy where:

> ...we are witnessing the early, turbulent days of a revolution as significant as any other in human history. A new medium of human communications is emerging, one that may prove to surpass all previous revolutions in its impact on our economic and social life. The computer is expanding from a tool for information management to a tool for communications.... In this digital economy, individuals and enterprises create wealth by applying knowledge, networked human intelligence, and effort to manufacturing, agriculture, and services. In the digital frontier of this economy, the players, dynamics, rules, and requirements for survival and success are changing.
>
> (Tapscott 1995: xiii)

Plus ça change? The impact of eBusiness on workplace design can also be viewed as a management fad which, like trends in music or clothes, go in and out of favour as consumer tastes change or people get older. Like management trends in general, the concept of eBusiness has just about reached the stage of popular critique and many would argue that it is only a matter of time before it is seen as a populist notion or fad more associated with youth culture than organisational logic. However, the concept of workplace design has a much deeper history, and as a popular practice has survived intact for over 50 years.

This chapter sets out to analyse the social and psychological impact of eBusiness, technology enhancements, and organisational change on the nature of work and employment. It takes as its focus how workplace design can be used to combine the physical work environment, technology and the flexible workforce in a more employee-centred manner. It therefore raises issues associated with facilities management in the new eBusiness environment.

Although globalism and the E-explosion of the 1990s have placed significant attention on the concept of the 'non-physical' workplace, there has been little research on the impact on facilities design for organisations. Systems of work which stress the significance of the Internet and the growing role of flexibility of work remain ill-defined and tend to focus attention on technology, knowledge management, and the need for 'rethinking' the organisation of the future. We argue here that a focus on human-computer interaction which emphasises the link between person and machine without considering the physical workplace is futuristic at best, and naïve in its conceptualisation of the brave new world. Organisations going through the change process of the 'E-age' will have to think radically about organisational form. However, a crucial mistake would be to deny the significance of the physical form through assertions of Internet supremacy. The management of eBusiness needs to analyse the impact on organisational structures, teamwork, and inter/intra-organisational collaborations. People need places to work and eBusiness, if it does anything, gives us an opportunity to examine how workplace design can be used to re-invigorate the corporation, providing us with new models of doing business and enjoying work.

In this chapter we look at a case study of workplace design with an eBusiness emphasis. The case allows us to explore the key issues in developing work organisations capable of managing flexible workforces. The emphasis is on what we term the 'corporate nomad', a form of flexible worker, whose needs are to combine technology advancement, temporal distortions, and team working. This chapter therefore focuses on the key issues organisations will need to take into account during the introduction of more flexible forms of work driven by technological and eBusiness concerns.

Workplace design: from the quality of working life to the eWorker

The boundaries of what management once considered acceptable work redesign have been expanded by burgeoning eBusiness technology combined with continuous competitive pressures. The approaches now being developed give employees considerably enhanced discretion and opportunities for skills development, lifestyle change and improved performance. However, are such assertions necessarily new? In the 1980s, Reich argued that rapid changes in the technology of products and production demanded the development of 'flexible systems' (1983). Market segmentation, increasingly informed and demanding consumers, complex and sophisticated product and process technologies, and changes in tastes and fashions, meant that speed and flexibility of response were going to be essential organisational characteristics. Hirschhorn (1984) argued that while modern organisational systems involved little manual work, the need for employee autonomy and problem-solving skills needed to be enhanced, and work reorganisation based on the socio-technical systems design approach would prove more effective. There may be a sense in which the concept of 'new wine in old bottles' appears appropriate for discussions of the impact of eBusiness on workplace design.

So what is new about the impact of eBusiness on design? Bradley and Woodling (2000) suggest that eBusiness, through the effective use of information and communications technologies (ICT), is having an impact on the way in which business space is managed;

> Most organisations are seeking to minimise fixed costs of business space and ICT infrastructure. However, they often need to rapidly accommodate fluctuations in number and locations of personnel (often project-based) for a restricted duration and ideally without incremental increase in support costs.
>
> (Bradley and Woodling 2000: 210)

Similarly, Sparrow (2000) suggests that:

> key organisational behaviours came to the fore in this teleworking environment. Companies began to shift their internal and external resourcing systems towards the assessment of important competencies such as information search, flexibility and problem generation skills.

eBusiness brings with it certain design issues which management need to face, including:

- how to manage knowledge and labour;
- how to manage the interaction between people in numerous workplaces in synchronous and asynchronous patterns;
- how to control organisations in non-traditional manners;
- how to manage closer relationships between the supplier, producer and consumer (both on a business-to-consumer and business-to-business basis);
- how to manage the integration between the information networks of customers and suppliers.

Renewed interest in work design is thus based on pressures arising from turbulent market conditions, and from the development of electronic business in manufacturing and services which encourage a reconsideration of work flows and work roles. This revival is not based directly on the 'quality of working life' but on less altruistic motives. These new pressures have created fresh and more pressing management problems, particularly with respect to the development of flexibility in organisations designed to deal with stability, and with lower levels of turbulence. Thus a climate of acceptability in relation to worker control has been established, in which management's perception of the legitimate boundaries of autonomy have been widened. Many organisations have felt these pressures and the response, in several instances, has been to look at ways of 'working smarter'. The reality of this is getting the best level of performance from individuals through employee involvement. One of the key success criteria associated with this is the creation of a work environment that embraces technology and the employee.

eBusiness, flexible customers and corporate nomads

The blurring of the buyer/supplier/customer relationship

If we define eBusiness as a combination of technologies, applications, processes, business strategies and practices necessary to do business electronically (Taylor and Berg 1995), then how does this affect the nature of the relationships between buyers and suppliers, and between organisations and their customers? eBusiness technologies such as the Internet have had a significant effect on business-to-consumer trading over the last 5 years. However, there appears to be an even greater potential associated with business-to-business transactions (Kehoe and Boughton 1998). Benjamin *et al.* (1986) argue that electronic commerce can reduce the costs of integrating customers and their suppliers, and that through electronic networks companies can achieve integration by tightly coupling processes at the interfaces between each stage of the value chain. The effective implementation of eBusiness to support supplier relationships and to optimise the supply chain requires that eBusiness is fully integrated into the business architecture and the technology infrastructure of both the supplier and the customer. eBusiness technologies are eliminating activities normally carried out in customer and supplier organisations. Such changes pose an immense challenge to the management of inter-organisational interactions. eBusiness is also having the effect of 'blurring' the traditional boundaries in the value chain between suppliers, manufacturers and end customers (McIvor *et al.* 2000). On a related theme, MIT's 'Management in the 1990s' research project differentiated Business Process Reengineering from Business Network Redesign (BNR). While the former focused attention on the redesign of internal organisational processes, the latter concerned itself with the wider business network (Peppard 1996). In a similar vein, McIvor *et al.* (2000) illustrate the importance of considering the inter-organisational processes between the customer and supplier. Grover and Malhotra (1997) suggest that the Internet will be a crucial device for the development of cross-functional team working across organisational boundaries. eBusiness automates transaction-type activities between buyers and suppliers; this enables those previously involved in such functions to concentrate on 'value-adding activities', such as the strategic development of buyer/supplier/customer relationships, knowledge management and new product development. Related to this is the fact that participants are being enabled to make more informed decisions through free access to wider information.

eBusiness design and the corporate nomad

A dynamic, cost-cutting, quality maximising business environment creates pressures on organisations to reduce fixed assets and minimise spending on buildings and facilities. However, this occurs at a time when businesses find it difficult to predict accurately future demand for products and services. Consequently, organisations need to accommodate fluctuations in the number and location of personnel for a restricted duration but in a way which does not lead to a concomitant increase in support costs. The challenge, as Bradley and Woodling (2000:162–3) suggest, is: 'How can alternative workplaces maintain the corporate values of identity, service and environmental quality as well as enabling rapidly assembled teams to form and perform effectively from the outset?' The management of facilities design brings with it a growing, unsatisfied demand for faster response, limited-duration business space and infrastructure.

Paralleling the change in the demand for business space usage is an eBusiness technology revolution which offers the advantages of:

- moving the concept and purpose of work towards the use and management of knowledge;
- temporal space reduction, enabling multiple projects/people/places interaction;
- loosening traditional management controls and hierarchies in favour of collaborative information sharing project processes;
- closer relationships between buyers/suppliers/customers;
- integration of information networks between customers and suppliers
- focusing on core business and outsourcing the rest

(Bradley and Woodling 2000:162–3).

eBusiness thus allows us to reformulate what we mean by the organisation and the workplace. The reformulation has two crucial aspects to it. First, for the individual charged with the challenge of working within an eBusiness environment, the concepts of space and time are different. We can visualise this individual as being capable of working independently of location and time. What these individuals need is access to their organisation as a 'club' in which to meet with other highly autonomous eBusiness collaborators (Worthington 1997).

Second, the workplace itself also needs to be reconstituted. Organisations need to

> ...rent access to facilities and resources wherever they may be, whenever needed. The ability to gain access 'anytime, anywhere', is a fundamental aspect of new ways of working, and a major attribute of the quality of place (the *genus loci*) in the new economy, in which speed of access will be the major provider of comparative advantage.
>
> (Bradley and Woodling 2000:162–3)

We can therefore envision the eBusiness as an organisation utilising a multimedia environment through computer supported collaborative work (CSCW) in project-based teams (thus *creating oases for corporate nomads*).

The impact of eBusiness on facilities management and design

It would be true to say that concern over the ability to provide organisations with infrastructure services management has generally been considered to be secondary to the delivery of an organisation's core business activities. However, as business has become ever more competitive, so there has been an increasing focus on the need to drive down the costs of doing business and to move beyond simple 'least cost' and 'non-core' evaluations of facilities management (FM) delivery. The design of space in the organisation has become relevant to business success in ways that many do not fully understand. The design of the working environment has for a long time been considered a marginal and technical matter, best left to experts to sort out. With the onset of eBusiness, changes in the ways in which organisations operate, are dependent upon attracting, retaining and stimulating people. This has increased awareness that FM needs to respond to organisational change (Becker 1990; Cairns and Beech 1999; Grimshaw 1999; Nutt 1999). Modern eBusinesses will need to strive to be more attractive to ordinary people. One crucial aspect of this attractiveness is the accessibility and functioning of office space. In general, the design of buildings has stayed, physically, more or less exactly where office design began at the beginning of the twentieth century. Facilities managers are inherently conservative, in spite of the fact that the concept of facilities management developed largely because of a growing realisation that the physical environment of the office was insufficient to fulfil rapidly developing business requirements. Duffy (2000) argues that facilities management is a static profession because of a set of fundamental beliefs concerning how people and buildings interact. These assume that:

> . . . an idle underclass has to be constantly supervised (the open plan); each step in career advancement within stable organisational hierarchies must always be marked (elaboration of grade and status); everyone needs to be constantly reminded who is on top (sharply differentiated space allocation); departments, functions and individuals should be kept apart (strict boundary maintenance); quasi-monopolies must control information flow (yet more boundary maintenance); presenteeism (as opposed to absenteeism) is always a good thing (a fixed desk for everyone all the time); home and work are two different and irreconcilable worlds (commuting is the natural state of mankind).

We have seen, throughout the eBusiness revolution, trends towards greater organisational flexibility coinciding with more intensive use of information technology. In the early 1990s a report involving twenty-two in-depth case studies in eight European countries, entitled *The Intelligent Building in Europe*, suggested that while the impact of IT on organisations and buildings has been enormous over the last 20 years, it would be regarded as a liberating rather than a constraining force during the next decade. 'It will allow greater flexibility of building usage and encourage new ways of working' (DEGW 1992: 17).

Just as the effective application of information technology is recognised as an essential resource for business, the DEGW study recognised the need for intelligent buildings that provide a responsive, effective and supportive environment within which the organisation could achieve its business objectives: 'building, space and business technologies are the tools that help this happen' (DEGW 1992: 5). This concept of 'building intelligence' was regarded as 'a collection of technologies able to respond to organisational change over time' (DEGW 1992: 5). Buildings as physical entities have, of course, no innate intelligence. However, effectively designed, equipped and managed environments can foster the conditions where the collective actions of individuals can more effectively generate, manipulate and distribute knowledge throughout the organisation and externally to customers and suppliers.

Drucker (1992) has suggested that knowledge is the primary resource for individuals and organisations. Specialised knowledge, he maintains, produces nothing. To be productive, knowledge must be integrated into a task. That is the purpose and function of organisation. Knowledge creating organisations invent knowledge not so much as a specialised activity but as a way of believing, a way of being in which everyone is a knowledge worker. Nonaka (1991) suggests that such institutions use organisational redundancy to focus thinking, encourage dialogue, and make tacit ideas explicit.

As technological developments have radically restructured business and revolutionised work processes, they have also liberated the individual. Individuals have greater access to knowledge and can share it more easily. Technology makes work accessible to the individual operating remotely, offering an unprecedented choice of flexible working options. For the organisation, ICT provides access to the increasingly scarce and highly skilled human resources necessary to thrive in the knowledge economy.

The increase in remote working enabled by mobile communications technologies also responds in part to the need to harness the power of knowledge by getting closer to customers. ICT gives workers the ability to collaborate while working in different places at the same time or at different times. Work is where you are when your are. Telecommuting does offer benefits to employees and employers, but not all workers are suited to teleworking. Isolation and a reduced sense of belonging are the key drawbacks identified by many authors (Tate 2000; Gordon 2000).

The blurring of the boundaries between social life and work life provide both opportunity and different types of stress on the individual. Organisations are, at the simplest level, collections of people, who through their combined efforts can achieve extraordinary results. Humans are essentially social animals whose psychological needs include those for social interaction, a sense of purpose and a sense of belonging. Offices are social spaces. The whole reason for their existence is as a place for people to meet and work together.

For some people, ICT allows them to work remotely and on the move; for the vast majority, the notion of a single workplace will remain. As our ability to generate and process information, at any time and in any place increases, organisational development will see more team-based working, flattening of hierarchies, empowerment and customer interactions. The fact is that work has changed dramatically over the last 10 years, yet workplace design has been slow to respond. Traditional office environments are already outdated and future work settings are likely to challenge our paradigms further.

What then might the future workplace look like? What we do know is that traditional office design is socio-fugal. It drives people into cellular offices at the expense of interaction. In the knowledge-based organisation people need to be able to come together and interact in teams. With less hierarchy and more open access to knowledge, the workplace becomes a catalyst for creativity.

Traditionally, offices have been used to confer status on individuals and to demonstrate the distribution of power within the organisation. (Barnard 1954; Katz and Khan 1978; Konar *et al.* 1982). We also know that the highest quality and greatest amount of space is usually reserved for the most senior staff who, conversely, spend the least amount of time there. In the future, knowledge workers will place increased demands for a more equitable allocation and distribution of space and resources. Traditional signs of status have included location (Steele 1973), accessibility (Langdon 1966), floorspace (Fetridge and Minor 1975), furnishings (Duffy 1969) and personalisation (Sundstrom 1986). In the knowledge-based organisation, where people are constantly changing their team-based structures, new ways will have to be found to confer rank or status where important. The high level of ability of a hospital nurse, for example, is indicated by a badge of rank on the hat.

We also know that use of space varies dramatically over the course of a typical day. At some times there are very low levels of occupancy in some locations and high intensity demand on others, such as meeting rooms. As companies move towards a more flexible cost base, contingency workers have become more common; organisational restructuring has seen an increase in contract-based staff to meet short-term changes in demand, in order to tailor services to meet customer requirements. The office of the future, therefore, needs to be flexible and adaptable to sudden changes in organisational demand.

Office design has recently begun to incorporate a range of alternative workplace strategies, including universal footprints (a standardised allocation of space which can be configured to a variety of different settings to meet the needs of individuals workstyles, or such space can be reconfigured to alternate uses such as meeting areas or libraries), multiple activity settings, non-territorial offices, shared assigned spaces, touchdown areas and hotelling. In addition, workplace strategies often encompass a wider range of off-site options, such as home working, telecommuting, virtual offices, satellite offices and the use of serviced office space.

Gordon (2000) highlights the fact that telecommuting is on a steady growth curve. Many employers are starting to divide work done in the traditional office versus work done elsewhere. The increasing army of 'corporate nomads' who spend time between offices, working from home or travelling, also require an oasis, a place to replenish supplies, gain access to resources, socially interact and share knowledge. However, many authors agree that the growth of teleworking has so far failed to live up to the expectation that it would become the new way to work. Tate (2000) highlights the fact that many people still continue commuting to the office. Charlton (1996) claims that teleworking will continue to grow slowly and that it will be restricted to niche markets.

In the age of the Internet, at the dawn of the knowledge-based society, it is strange that we tolerate buildings—and building environment systems—that assume that everyone comes in at nine and leaves at five, and sits continuously at a desk for 5 days a week. The model, of course, is still the factory, where foremen had to put enormous emphasis on synchrony to force a barely literate proletariat to work at the loom and the lathe. When the bell rings the work begins. When the siren blows it is over—for the day. The reality of eBusiness working life is far more complex. There are aspects of managing knowledge and time that create greater degrees of individual independence, yet place a higher value on inter and intra-organisational teamwork. This suggests that 'ubiquitous networks mean that the office is wherever we want it to be' (Duffy 2000: 3).

The following case study demonstrates the integration of strategic real estate management with business planning and the design of the working environment. Office design can play a pivotal role in supporting new ways of working. This case recognises that, after people and knowledge, space is a major organisational resource that must be managed efficiently and imaginatively if it is to be used to maximum advantage.

ABC gets real (estate)

Opportunities to rethink the way in which the working environment supports an organisation arise in response to either business or real estate triggers. The two, however, should not be seen as mutually exclusive, but rather as inter-related dimensions that collectively affect organisational performance.

Real estate triggers, such as lease breaks, focus attention on considerations such as space and image related requirements, technological requirements, and the need for real estate flexibility in line with dynamic business needs. Each of these has a bottom line impact through the costs of facilities to be provided.

Business triggers might include changes in staff numbers or structure, company mergers and acquisitions, changes in customer expectations, new product offerings, and investments in new technologies. Each of these may entail specific real estate requirements.

Despite the fact that offices are available 365 days per year, by the time the working pattern has been reduced to a five-day week, an eight-hour day and staff have gone on holiday, had lunch, been ill and visited clients, buildings are used for less than 10 per cent of their full potential. The pressure to maximise the potential of space by increasing staff density is understandable. The potential exists to reduce costs by reviewing and changing working patterns, and by designing working environments that reflect these.

ABC was one of the world's largest media services groups, employing more than 30,000 staff in over 50 countries. In 1996 the group introduced a new workplace programme which provided guidance to all group companies on best practice in real estate management and space planning. The programme was developed in response to a realisation that, after people, the group invested more money worldwide in real estate than anything else.

An internal team of specialist workplace consultants and designers was set up to administer and implement the workplace programme worldwide. Three teams had geographic responsibility for the Americas, Europe, and Asia Pacific respectively, and each team was responsible for providing strategic advice to individual companies on areas ranging from real estate acquisitions or disposals to workplace relocation and reconfiguration.

Each team had to be extremely flexible in order to respond to the needs of individual business units, which themselves operated in a particularly dynamic industry—no more so than in the Asia Pacific region. Operating across significantly different time zones, the teams made use of videoconferencing for design team meetings, and would transfer data and drawings electronically to the European office for ongoing development at the end of the Asian working day. Collectively, the teams had the capacity for 24-hour working on time critical projects. The teams were highly mobile and autonomous, and spent little time in a single location. As such the workplace consultancy teams were virtual operations in every sense of the word. They were, in fact, a microcosm of many elements of the operational structure of the larger group companies.

While the drivers for organisational change vary for any company, a number of factors characterised the Asia Pacific business of the group. First, real estate cycles tended to be significantly shorter than those in Europe; typically office leases were only for 3 years. Further, most office developments were speculator designed. In rapidly developing economies investment in speculative office developments could quickly lead to an oversupply situation, increasing tenant choice and driving down rental costs. Often rental savings between locations could offset the costs of moving to new offices, including fitting out.

In cities, such as Hong Kong, Shanghai, Auckland, Sydney, Mumbai and New Delhi, up to ten companies from the group operated from independent locations. Opportunities existed therefore to co-locate companies, pooling the overall space requirement and deriving both financial benefits from economies of scale, but also organisational and operational synergies from being together.

A pervasive characteristic of office use in all locations analysed by the workplace consultancy was that, increasingly, staff spent less time in the office and more time travelling or in alternative office arrangements. Hong Kong, in addition to servicing a significant market in its own right, acted as the Asia Pacific regional headquarters for each of the group companies. A high proportion of staff spent a significant amount of their time travelling and working from other locations. A further characteristic of businesses such as advertising, marketing, and public relations was their primary concern with the communication of information or ideas to enable people to make choices about what to buy, about their lifestyles, about health matters or how to vote, etc.

The development of communications products relied heavily upon teamwork to allow the exchange of ideas and information from a variety of sources and to transform these ideas into a communications strategy. The client and the consumer were also integral parts of the production process.

Whilst ICT enabled new ways of communicating and working, it was not in itself the main reason for organisational change and workplace redesign;

customers, competition and change were the primary change drivers. Getting closer to customers and involving them in the supply chain, maintaining competitive advantage, and being flexible, adaptable and responsive could be achieved through the creation of an enabling business infrastructure.

The Hong Kong Co-location project provided an opportunity for the group to optimise returns from real estate as a factor of production. Within a period of 12 months, ten group companies would reach lease expiry points at a time when the Hong Kong office market was in a substantial oversupply situation. The Asian economies had recently slowed and a number of companies were experiencing a period of consolidation or negative growth. The group also wanted to use the workplace reconfiguration exercise as a means of introducing and implementing a wider programme of new work practices, in particular to improve organisational communications and facilitate teamwork, and to gain synergies from merging back-office operations.

The workplace consultants wanted to create environments that provided more flexible and effective use of space in order to accommodate changes in organisational demand over the medium term. In addition, the environment needed to be branded to reflect the culture of each company to visitors and employees. In every case the organisational analysis was an organisational intervention aimed at exploring the art of the possible in terms of existing working practices and how they could be improved upon. To this end the intervention focused on the interrelationship between people, process and place over time.

Employee education and communications were seen as a fundamental output of the exercise. It was insufficient merely to undertake organisational and building research and then implement a design solution. The resultant design solutions would have to have a high degree of employee ownership following significant input and 'education' into new ways of working. As such the exercise could be regarded as an opportunity for organisational learning.

Office environments were reconfigured as multiple activity settings that better reflected the way in which the workplace provided support to the individual and the team. The reconfigurations allocated space by task and function rather than rank or status. Areas were provided for formal and informal meetings, stimulating brainstorming tanks; visibility and circulation routes were redesigned to provide greater opportunities for chance encounters. Social spaces such as cybercafes, libraries and staff clubs were created to enhance the sense of cohesion and teamwork within the office. Settings were designed to meet work requirements ranging from quiet concentration to noisy and humorous brainstorming. The workspaces included opportunities for hotdesking, touchdown areas, hotelling and bookable and non-bookable meeting areas. While the consultancy and design teams encountered inevitable cultural barriers, the opportunity to implement alternative workplace strategies was welcomed and embraced.

The success in introducing workplace change was not, however, just due to the development of eBusiness and ICT. It was about developing an appreciation of the way in which the workplace supported the organisation and the individual. The new workplace configurations had to be seen to be equitable. As Becker (1981) has suggested, the concept of equity, one of the basic principles of space standards, may be enhanced through variety which provides individuals, who differ in work style or level of competence, with a range of environmental supports to suit the diversity of individual needs. Equity from the employee perspective was not defined in terms of having the same amount of something. Equity became defined as the provision of appropriate environmental supports for a given level of activity and knowledge. All design processes involved a series of trade-offs. The accommodation of diversity created environments that were both flexible and resilient. However, end user involvement in workplace design was a fundamental component in design solution acceptability.

Conclusions

Awareness that technology alone cannot provide eBusiness with the solutions to organisational dilemmas is growing. McLoughlin and Clark (1994) argue that technology has created an imperative in which cognitive skills are at a premium and that this encourages multi-skilled team working. eBusiness will certainly enhance the concept of team working as ICT-supported collaboration is increased, but the concept of the virtual team—how it is formed and maintained—still requires much research.

If knowledge is the fundamental currency of the modern business, then the ability to share and manipulate it cannot be realised through investment in ICT alone. The new workplace must accommodate a much wider variety of settings than those provided by traditional design solutions. Not all work happens at a desk. Not all meetings take place in meeting rooms. Knowledge workers need a variety of different settings to suit their different needs at different times of the day. They need places for individuals to think and work quietly, places for groups to gather and exchange ideas, places for people to meet—which may be formal or informal, scheduled or impromptu, electronically or face to face—places for teams to set up long-term projects, and places for those just dropping in.

The success of alternative workplace strategies is ultimately measured by their contribution towards increased organisational effectiveness, often measured in terms of the organisation bottom line. But organisational effectiveness might also be measured in terms of an organisation's general state of health. The ability to achieve goals, the presence or absence of organisational stress, the quality of life of staff, the capacity to be flexible, adaptable and resilient to change.

Enabling technologies often play a key role in harnessing the potential of truly flexible working, providing access to information regardless of location. Workplace flexibility in the ABC case study was achieved not through investment in enabling technologies but through an in-depth analysis and understanding of the functioning of the business and the way in which the physical environment supports it. Many of the most fundamental tasks in a knowledge-based organisation are in fact 'low-tech'—tasks such as thinking, social interaction and generating ideas, the act of being creative.

Increasingly, facilities are being seen as a factor of production and business resource rather than a corporate overhead. As with any factor of production, they must work for the business and allow companies to release the potential of the workforce. While an organisation's needs are inherently dynamic, physical facilities are, by contrast, relatively static and have often been regarded as slow to respond to the needs of business.

The notion of the virtual workplace—any time, any place—pervades the language surrounding eBusiness. The stark reality, however, is that the office provides us with a physical touchstone amidst the virtual reality of modern business. The workplace provides us with a sense of place, a sense of belonging, an oasis, and in some cases the office might be construed as a metaphor for the corporate entity itself: purposeful, collegiate, social, resilient and flexible.

Nobody knows what a better workplace might look like. The responsibility of designers and managers should therefore be to help organisations manage their workplace experiments more intelligently. Albert Einstein once said that 'Imagination is more powerful than Knowledge'. Despite all the knowledge we might have of business and human needs, unless we can imagine a better workplace, how can we design one?

References

Barnard, C. (1954) 'Functional pathology of status systems in formal organisations', in W. Whyte (ed.) *Industry and Society*, Chicago: McGraw Hill.

—— (1981) *Workspace: creating environments in organisations*, New York: Praeger.

Becker, F.D. (1990) *The Total Workplace: facilities management and the elastic organisation*, New York: Van Nostrand Reinhold.

Benjamin, R.I., Malone, W.T. and Yates, J. (1986) 'Electronic markets and electronic hierarchies', CISR Working Paper No. 137, *Centre for Information Systems Research*, Boston, MA: Sloan School of Management, Massachusetts Institute of Technology.

Bradley, S. and Woodling, G. (2000), 'Accommodating future business intelligence: new workspace and work-time challenges for management and design', *Facilities*, 18: 3–4.

Cairns, G. and Beech, N. (1999), 'Flexible working: organisational liberation or individual straitjacket', *Facilities*, 17: 1–2.

Charlton, J. (1996) 'Home or away', *Computer Weekly*, May.

DEGW (1992) *The Intelligent Building In Europe: study report*, May, DEGW and Teknibank.

Drucker, P. (1992) 'The New Society of organisations', *Harvard Business Review*, Sept–Oct.

Duffy, F. (1969) 'Role and status in the office', *Architectural Association Quarterly*, 1.

—— (2000) 'Design and facilities management in a time of change', *Facilities*, 18: 10–12.

Fetridge, C. and Minor, R. (eds) (1975) *Office Administration Handbook*, Chicago: Dartnell Press.

Gordon, G. (2000) 'Administration and General Information FAQ', *Internet—Telecommuting Tools*.

Grimshaw, R.W. (1999) 'The wider implications of managing change', *Facilities*, 17: 1–2.

Grover, V. and Malhotra, M. (1997), 'Business process re-engineering: a tutorial on the concept, evolution, method, technology and application', *Journal of Operations Management*, 15.

Hirschhorn, L. (1984) *Beyond Mechanisation*, Cambridge, Mass: MIT Press.

Katz, D. and Khan, R. (1978) *The Social Psychology of Organisations*, New York: Wiley.

Kehoe, D.F. and Boughton, N.J. (1998) 'DOMAIN: dynamic operations management across the Internet', in *Strategic Management of the Value Chain*, sponsored by the International Federation for Information Processing, University of Strathclyde.

Konar, E., Sundstrom, E., Brady, C., Mandel, D. and Rice R. (1982) 'Status markers in the office', *Environment and Behaviour*, 14, 3.

Langdon, F. (1966) 'Modern offices: a user survey', *National Building Studies Research Paper*, London: HMSO.

McIvor, R., Humphreys, P. and Huang, G. (2000) 'Electronic commerce: re-engineering the buyer-supplier interface', *Business Process Management Journal*, 6: 2.

McLoughlin, I. and Clark, J. (1994) *Technological Change at Work*, Milton Keynes: Open University Press.

Nonaka, I. (1991) 'The knowledge creating company', *Harvard Business Review*, Nov–Dec.

Nutt, B. (1999) 'Linking FM practice and research', *Facilities*, 17: 1–2.

Peppard, J. (1996) 'Broadening visions of business process reengineering', *Omega*, 24: 3.

Reich, R.B. (1983) *The Next American Frontier*, New York: Times Books.

Sparrow, P.R. (2000) 'New employee behaviours, work design and forms of work organisation: what is in store for the future of work?', *Journal of Managerial Psychology*, 15: 3.

Steele, F. (1973) *Physical Settings and Organisational Development*, Reading, MA: Addison Wesley.

Sundstrom, E. (1986) *Work Places: the psychology of the physical environment in offices and factories*, Cambridge: Cambridge University Press.

Tapscott, D. (1995) *The Digital Economy: promise and peril in the age of networked intelligence*, London: McGraw-Hill.

Tate, R. (2000) 'The real virtual office', *BA Business Life*, London: Premier Media Partner Ltd.

Taylor, D. and Berg, T. (1995) 'The business value of electronic commerce', *Strategic Analysis Report*, Stanford, CT.: Gartner Group.

Worthington, J. (ed.) (1997) *Reinventing the Workplace*, Oxford: Butterworth-Heinemann.

3 Organisational structures for eBusiness

Some marketing challenges

Lisa Harris

Introduction

The 1990s have witnessed an increasing trend towards new forms of organisational structure, a process facilitated by developments in information technology such as the Internet. These developments are presenting novel and interesting challenges for marketers in the early years of the new millennium. This chapter is based upon the results of an international research project that examined inter-organisational networks in three European countries: the UK, Germany and Denmark. It begins by highlighting the need for structural change in the eBusiness era, and then examines how organisational structures have evolved over time. The characteristics of 'virtual', 'networked' and 'clicks and mortar' organisations are then described as examples of new structural types. The nature and extent of the challenges posed for marketers within such organisations are discussed throughout, and data from a number of contemporary case studies are drawn upon to demonstrate how such challenges may be met. The chapter concludes by speculating on what the future holds for these organisations and whether the new models described here are likely to offer significant competitive advantage over more traditionally organised operations.

The need for new organisational structures

Internet developments are currently providing a powerful incentive for established firms to experiment with new ways of organising their operations, in order to compete with more flexible new market players that are not burdened by legacy computer systems and entrenched operational routines. For example, Kalakota and Robinson put consideration of new forms of organisational structure at the heart of eBusiness strategy:

> Maintaining the status quo is not a viable option. Unfortunately too many companies develop a pathology of reasoning, learning and attempting to

innovate only in their comfort zones. The first step to seeing differently is to understand that eBusiness is about structural transformation.

(Kalakota and Robinson 1999: 5)

This unequivocal statement is supported by Stroud who claims:

The benefits that the Internet is expected to deliver will not be realised unless a company adapts its organisational structure and methods to meet the radical new ways of working that this new technology makes possible.

(Stroud 1998: 225)

Day (1998) notes that many firms try to maintain traditional structures when developing their online strategies, and hence become victims of new firms with better alignments of structure and strategy. Effective eBusiness strategy, however, calls for a re-engineering of processes and structures in order to focus on key customer groups, rather than product or service divisions. It also implies a need for cross-functional team working. As Siegel warns:

The customer-led company has a broad interface across which all employees can get to know their customers. Employees invite customers in to collaborate on new products, support systems, and methodologies ... Facilitating those interactions will take new communication skills, new tools, and the ability to move people in and out of product teams easily.

(Siegel 2000: 35)

Furthermore, even such radical restructuring cannot be regarded as just a one-off activity. Firms looking to remain competitive in the eBusiness arena have to be prepared to reorganise and restructure themselves more or less continuously.[1] As discussed in more detail elsewhere (Jackson and Harris 2000), if the restructuring of traditional businesses really is so central to their development of successful eBusiness strategies, it is essential they understand how to manage change effectively in order to sustain competitive advantage. This is because it is easier for a newly formed organisation to operate in 'virtual' or 'networked' ways than it is to impose massive organisational change upon a long established, hierarchical and inflexible organisation. This important point is demonstrated in the next section, which provides a brief review of historical developments in organisational structure.

Organisational structure: a brief history

Organisational structure was once the way in which companies could control the flow of information within the firm. Clear hierarchies of responsibility meant that information flowed slowly up and down functional areas, but was often not made available to other parts of the organisation, or could be excluded from certain individuals. An individual's position in the management hierarchy could be ascertained by the degree of access they held to important information. Powerful fiefdoms could be established by individuals who controlled access to such information. With the recent development of the Internet, together with internal company 'intranets', such barriers to information access can now be transcended. Real-time access to information is available to any employee with Internet access, and the activities of diverse functional areas become transparent to employees at all hierarchical levels. On the other hand, the sheer volume of information now available to organisations creates problems of its own. These developments have major implications for marketers seeking opportunities to generate competitive advantage; the relevant issues raised by changes in the way organisations can be structured are explored in later sections.

Since the pioneering work of Burns and Stalker (1961) it has been accepted that unpredictable business environments may require 'organic' organisational structures, rather than the more traditional 'mechanistic' forms best suited to more stable conditions. An example of a 'mechanistic' structure would be the hierarchical and functionally divided arrangements still common in long-established organisations such as banks. An example of an 'organic' structure would be the creation of flexible cross-functional project teams within a firm to develop specific new products as the occasion demands. The assumption here is that such organisations can generate a high degree of 'fit' between the external environment and the internal organisational form. However, the scenario of organic structures enabling 'matching' to take place with changing external conditions is increasingly problematic for several reasons. First, the capacity to understand the requirements of the external environment is seen as relatively straightforward. Second, the boundary between the external environment and the organisation is assumed to be clear and distinct. Finally, the achievement of optimum 'fit' is regarded as a stable and sustainable configuration. Miles and Snow (1986) criticised this model by noting how the external environment was becoming an ever-more dynamic and complex phenomenon. At the same time, boundaries between the organisation and its environment are becoming increasingly blurred. New forms of organisational structure that can be conceptualised as 'virtual', 'network' or 'clicks and mortar' organisations seek to address these drawbacks, and are described in the next section.

New forms of organisational structure

The catalyst for many recent changes in the structure of organisations is, of course, information technology. When this critical feature is taken together with general business trends towards reduced management hierarchies, de-bureaucratisation, team-based working and inter-organisational collaboration, then opportunities for entirely new ways of working across both time and space are created. One such innovation is teleworking, where employees may work from home or specialist regional centres rather than from a central office location. The UK Directory Enquiries service provides a good example of how callers can now be automatically routed to BT employees, working from home, who can access all the necessary data stored on a CD Rom.

Other examples of virtual organisations include software development companies that have considerably enhanced their productivity by creating new product development teams with representatives in the Far East, Middle East, Europe and America. Software development can thus be passed electronically around the world on a 24-hour basis; as the working day comes to an end in one particular centre, it will still be lunchtime in the next! Taking the degree of 'virtuality' to new extremes, some organisations now require no physical presence at all. A current example concerns a company with which the author is working; it has been set up under the control of one individual to provide data-warehousing and analysis services to retailers. The owner out-sources all of the product development, marketing and administrative functions to different organisations as required. The organisation therefore has no permanent staff, no geographic location and no expensive infrastructure. It can therefore compete effectively with the major market players on price.

The latest form of virtual organisation to make waves has been the emergence of 'meta-mediaries' which help their customers navigate the increasingly complex and rapidly changing world of the Internet. The costs associated with searching for and sorting relevant information are now so high that specialist firms are emerging to fulfil this role. While 'extranets' (which are extensions of company intranets to include customers and/or suppliers) are, on the one hand, short-circuiting traditional supply chains, on the other they are creating new market opportunities for intermediaries to help organisations to filter, control and manage the volume of information to which they are exposed. The most well-known example of a virtual organisation must be Amazon.com, which has no physical retail presence but has revolutionised the book selling market by linking directly with customers through an extensive and interactive website. For every middleman cut out of the value chain, however, new ones are created. Amazon now relies heavily upon business partners for services such as warehousing and advertising.

Another enormously successful virtual organisation is Edmunds.com. which acts as a 'one stop shop' for the automobile market. The firm has redrawn market boundaries by grouping together related services online such as spare parts, leasing facilities, insurance and car dealerships in 'seamless bundles' with a customer perspective. In the 'real' world, such organisations may inhabit different industry groups and sources of information are consequently fragmented. Edmunds collects referral fees from the connections made between customers and service providers, and with 80,000 'hits' per day, can provide a highly targeted audience for advertisers. The firm maintains its central position in the webs that it creates by broking connections between buyers (for example, by setting up special interest groups for classic cars) and also between sellers (for example, by linking finance companies with car dealerships). As such, both Edmunds and Amazon can also be regarded as classic examples of 'networked' organisations, defined as 'hybrids' of several firms working together for mutual benefit.

While there are undoubtedly many firms that have an established tradition of successful inter-organisational networking, recent Internet developments have made such initiatives increasingly central to eBusiness strategy. According to a special report on Business and the Internet in the *Economist* (1999):

> The first and most crucial shift in thinking is to get away from the idea that any business is more or less a free-standing entity. The objective for large companies must be to become e-business hubs and for smaller ones to ensure they are vital spokes. The companies involved must be willing to bring suppliers and customers deep into their processes and to develop a similar understanding of their business partners' processes. That implies a degree of openness and transparency which is new to most commercial organisations.

This warning is endorsed in the same publication by Symonds:

> The ability to collaborate with others may be just as much of a competitive advantage as the ability to deploy the technology. Certainly the technology matters, but getting the business strategy right matters even more. And that may mean not just re-engineering your company, but reinventing it.
>
> (Symonds 1999: 72)

Kalakota and Robinson (1999: 18) believe that the business design of the future will consist of a flexible network of relationships between firms, with customers and suppliers creating '*unique business organisms*'. Such structures enable resources to be pooled and hence generate economies of scale, with each network member contributing its particular expertise. It might be argued that these strategies are not new, and represent little more than the outsourcing of non-core activities to reduce costs. Kalakota and Robinson, however, argue that enthusiastic protagonists are going much further; changing corporate cultures, accessing key skills and implementing sophisticated technological systems in a manner that no individual firm could achieve alone.

At an early stage of the Internet era, Tapscott (1995) predicted the creation of competitive advantage in a digital world through collaboration, as networks of enterprises generate efficiencies for the benefit of all parties. In his most recent work (Tapscott *et al.* 2000) he is unequivocal about the value of such networks which he terms 'Business Webs' or 'B-webs':

> Business webs are inventing new value propositions, transforming the rules of competition, and mobilising people and resources to unprecedented levels of performance. Managers must master a new agenda for b-web strategy if they intend to win in the new economy.
>
> (Tapscott *et al.* 2000: 17)

Turner (2000) also emphasises how the development of the information economy (in particular, the transition from 'market-places' to 'market spaces' without the need for physical contact) is pushing firms towards organisational structures based on networks. As an example of how networking strategies are transforming organisational structures, Anders (2000) describes how Wells Fargo Bank is creating synergies by teaming with a number of small Internet firms. The bank prefers to learn from the new mindsets and high energy levels of such enterprises, rather than smothering creativity by trying to foster innovation within its own bureaucratic structures and the associated slow decision-making systems. From an Internet firm's perspective, valuable credibility can be obtained through association with a trusted brand in the banking world.

Some years ago, both Aoki (1984) and DeBresson and Amesse (1991) noted the growth of inter-organisational networking, especially in terms of risk-reduction strategies in increasingly unstable global markets. Networked organisational forms respond to the new complexity and rate of product innovation required by external environments by focusing internal organisation on distinctive competencies, while outsourcing non-distinctive activities. Another rationale for network formation is that synergies can be created by collaboration that would not be available to any one partner firm if acting alone. Van Rossum and Hicks (1996) showed that over time this strategy results in the emergence of collaborative networks, comprised of loosely coupled and autonomous organisational units both internal and external to the firm. In these circumstances boundaries within and between organisations become blurred, and resource flows between different network elements are based upon contractual mechanisms or even informal exchanges.

Networked structures permit organisational flexibility in the face of rapidly changing environmental conditions, and therefore represent a more viable response to the current business operating conditions than the 'organic' structures described earlier. In its simplest form, one party to a collaboration may obtain access to particular skills that it does not maintain in-house, while the other party is able to 'piggy-back' access to new markets that it would otherwise have found difficult to penetrate. In more complex cases, it may be difficult to ascertain the position of organisational boundaries, particularly if an organisation is involved in a number of different networks that change composition and evolve over time. In some industries, customers may be attracted to the network on the basis of the quality of the partner organisations involved (note for example, the often proudly displayed logo 'IBM Business Partner'). Such desirability can lead to the rather bizarre situation of firms 'competing to collaborate'. In this environment, traditional models of competition and industry structure, such as those espoused by Porter (1980), appear somewhat inadequate.

Harris (1999) describes how the key challenge for marketers at the strategic level lies in appreciating the extent of the difficulties inherent in building and maintaining successful networks. Networked organisations do not just 'happen' by themselves. To begin with, suitable partners have to be chosen. Even if a 'win-win' situation between collaborators is evident, the relationship between the partners still has to be nurtured and managed over time, if trust is to be developed and the firms are to work together effectively. Some difficult questions may have to be faced, such as what happens if an aggrieved partner tries to sabotage the network? Should a partner firm try to act in the interests of the network as a whole, or take whatever opportunities arise to maximise its own position within the network? Formal legal agreements are often deemed necessary to set out the respective obligations of the partners, especially in the early stages of a relationship. Formal arrangements may be relaxed as trust becomes established. On the other hand, the costs associated with managing the network may become so great as to negate the benefits of participation. It is often necessary to rely on key individuals with the power, vision and commitment to making partnerships work. While IBM now talks of the need for 'triple hybrid' managers to manage collaborative relationships effectively, the skills of the network broker can extend even further to encompass those of an entrepreneur, technician, sociologist, businessman and politician! In some cases, an independent 'network broker' may play a critical role in finding suitable partners, reconciling vested interests within the network and negotiating how network benefits are to be shared between the participants.

Piercy (1997) warns that a firm's marketing strategy must not be too susceptible to a failure in key networks. In other words, it is dangerous to become so dependent on the contribution of partners that the firm can no longer meet customer needs by itself. For historical reasons, collaborating with competitors did not come naturally for UK firms, but one of our case-study firms has successfully pursued strategies of inter-firm collaboration for many years. It provides a good endorsement of research by Dickson *et al.* (1997) which showed that companies involved in successful inter-organisational networking may become 'strategic collaborators' by internalising these networking skills and then applying them in entirely new contexts. The problem is that the firm now has no alternative to networking, because the particular skills needed to operate independently are no longer held in house. (See Coles and Harris (2001) for full details of this case study.)

Another challenge concerns how best to deal with collaborators who may also be competitors in other contexts. Seth and Sisodia (1999) use the term 'co-opetition' to describe such arrangements. Traditional marketing relationships focus upon five key groups, namely shareholders, employees, customers, suppliers and the community at large (see, for example, McIntosh *et al.* 1998). Competitors are usually conspicuous by their absence from such lists of potential stakeholders. A wider definition of stakeholders would include 'any group or individual who can affect or is affected by the corporation' (Freeman 1997). According to this definition, a competitor would clearly be a stakeholder of the firm, but the assumption of a competitive rather than collaborative environment remains the norm. In an influential article Hamel, Doz and Prahalad (1989: 67) advocate strategic alliances and networking between firms with their proposal that collaboration rather than competition is a winning strategy. They conclude that firms benefiting from competitive collaboration see it as competition in a different form. They regard harmony as the most important measure of success, co-operation as limited and learning from partners as paramount. Key challenges here include the ability to define the boundary between competition and collaboration, in other words being able to ascertain where the 'internal environment' becomes the 'external environment'.

At the operational level, one of the challenges marketers must meet with regard to Web-based inter-organisational networks is that customer communications do not necessarily involve just one customer talking to one enterprise. To provide the kind of service that improves the chance of customer loyalty, companies need to co-ordinate their partners and vendors and customers through extranets that facilitate the sharing of information across company boundaries. Kalakota and Robinson (1999) suggest considering partners and vendors to be part of the firm's extended enterprise, and this means sharing customer communication issues with everyone in contact with the customer through *integrated applications* such as customer service, field service, sales and marketing. This recommendation is endorsed by a global technology firm, with which the author is working, which believes such integration to be the most critical issue currently facing 'clicks and mortar' firms in developing a successful eBusiness strategy. Such open policies of information sharing mean a whole host of issues have to be addressed concerning the 'ownership' of customer data, notwithstanding the technical difficulties inherent in integrating computer systems belonging to different organisations.

Another operational challenge is the practical organisation of marketing functions and activities within an inter-firm network. Decisions need to be taken on where responsibility lies for particular tasks, to avoid duplication and customer confusion. In one of our case-study networks, four separate organisations were involved in a particular project; some employees reported to a manager who worked for another organisation, who in turn reported to an individual from a third organisation. When the project was running smoothly the arrangement worked well, but over time one of the partner firms became very unpopular and the relationships between individuals reporting to the managers from the maverick organisation became acrimonious and eventually unworkable.

'Clicks and mortar' organisational structures

Firms such as WH Smith (whsmith.co.uk) exemplify the trend towards 'clicks and mortar' operations, whereby synergies can be generated by the availability of a choice of delivery mechanisms through both traditional and Internet channels. Stores in prime high-street locations throughout the country can promote special Internet dealing offers, provide terminal access to online ordering for products not held in store, and also act as a collection point for returned goods that were delivered direct to the home. Nadler and Tushman (1999) note how the current business environment will require organisations to develop different kinds of structures in order to manage different channels of distribution simultaneously. Many firms are struggling with the concept of channel 'cannibalisation', whereby adding Internet-based channels to the market merely adds to costs by offering more choice to existing customers instead of attracting additional business. For example, RS Components has won many awards for the significant investment made in its innovative and highly successful website, but the firm admits that the volume of paper catalogues it produces has merely stabilised, and not decreased as might be expected.[2] Kumar (1999) reports that companies tend to use existing distribution networks for too long, fearing the wrath of powerful resellers within the channel. The temptation of course is not to 'rock the boat', but the opportunities for firms who are proactive in their consideration of electronic routes to market are considerable.

Debenhams is currently devoting considerable attention to its Internet channel. The firm has set up a separate eBusiness Division that is known internally as the 'pressure cooker', a reference to the prevailing frantic office atmosphere. Kleindl (2001) notes that such separate eBusiness divisions allow the firm to avoid conflicts between existing entrenched cultures and the new 'knowledge' mindset necessary for eBusiness success. By functioning as a totally separate unit the new division is 'ringfenced' from the established, slow-moving and inflexible bureaucracy of its parent, while still benefiting from association with a trusted brand image. In the current climate of 'dotcom' failures, the reputation and values associated with the traditional Debenhams brand are a powerful strategic asset. Indeed, many employees who left the company for the likes of Lastminute.com at the height of 'dot-com' mania in late 1999 are now trying to return. Debenhams.co.uk currently represents more secure employment prospects, a rising share price and solid financial backing from the parent company. British Airways is another high-profile organisation that recently set up a separate eBusiness division in order to mimic the speedy decision-making and organisational flexibility of an Internet start-up company.

The prospects for 'clicks and mortar' firms have also been enhanced with the recent news that Borders.com (supported by a rapidly growing network of high-street stores with coffee bar and browsing facilities) has overtaken Amazon.com (still resolutely virtual with no high-street representation) as the number one online bookseller, according to research by Forrester reported in The Sunday Times (10 December 2000). The report suggests that 'clicks and mortar' booksellers have already gained ground in areas such as customer service, and could benefit further with new online book buyers attracted to local store return and exchange facilities that the 'online-only' stores cannot offer. It recommends that Amazon seeks a partnership with an 'offline' retailer in order to sustain its market position.[3]

The dangers of Internet-only structures are highlighted by recent adverse publicity surrounding Easyrentacar.com. Cope (2000), writing for The Independent, is scathing about the standard of customer service offered by the company. Easyrentacar prides itself on the low prices it is able to charge through focusing solely on its Internet service, meaning that there is not even so much as a telephone helpline to handle customer queries. Even email responses are standardised, with computers sending prepared replies generated by key words in the text, which may not exactly conform to the enquirer's request. If the trend towards 'clicks and mortar' companies offering a multi-channel service described above is apparently paying dividends, it would make sense for online-only operations to offer some services that are also rooted in the physical world.

For established firms looking to add online channels to market, some of the marketing challenges are internal. As highlighted at the beginning of the chapter, significant organisational change may be involved and effective com-munication within the firm of the need for change—and the role of employees in effecting it—is essential to ensure staff commitment. Supporters, neutrals and opponents of change need to be identified and communications phrased appropriately to each group. It is particularly vital to ensure 'buy-in' from key decision-makers and potential project champions. If the project also involves the development of cross-functional or inter-organisational networks, then clear communication of the way things are done, respective responsibilities and project objectives, takes on even more importance. Other challenges concern how to integrate 'online' and 'offline' marketing strategies to ensure commonality of message and to create synergies. A simple example of such integration concerns the use of 'call-back' buttons where a customer can request, through the website, a telephone call from a salesperson in order to discuss the purchase request in more detail.

There are other practical marketing issues to consider. Customer expectations are rising; many now expect an immediate response to queries at any time of the day or night, and are unimpressed if the website does not display the most up-to-date product information and availability. This puts pressure on firms to ensure customer service centres are adequately staffed, and that their sites are easy to navigate and contain the information that the customer seeks. For 'clicks and mortar' firms that are still also committed to customer interaction, either face to face or by telephone, there can be a significant additional cost associated with providing an extra channel to market. There are also implications for the way in which marketing departments are staffed in terms of the allocation of 'online' and 'offline' duties and the additional training requirements necessary.

The traditional organisation of marketing departments is by means of geography (which of course is limited in importance on the Web) or by product. In the latter case it is difficult to implement strategies of personalisation and cross-selling which cross product-line boundaries. Organisation by customer group makes the most sense in terms of personalising interactions and assessing lifetime customer value, strategies which Internet developments are rapidly facilitating. Individual customers can now be tracked regardless of their physical location or specific product choices. Firms such as Amazon can track wide ranging purchases back to a single customer account, and customise future promotional campaigns and cross-selling opportunities accordingly. However, for 'clicks and mortar' firms that often lack sophisticated and integrated computer systems, these developments require a feel for the whole product range and geographic spread of the business that is beyond the scope of an individual marketer, and also challenge the organisation's internal communication effectiveness. To address these difficulties, Hanson (2000) recommends the sharing of information through intranets, extranets and the Web itself, so that staff can acquire, update and develop the customer profiles necessary for relationship building campaigns to work efficiently. Achrol (1991) also suggests that marketing, in this sense of information exchange or relationship building, will play a central organising role in the development of effective eBusiness strategies.

From this brief review it is clear that marketing has an important role to play in the eBusiness era, although perhaps not with the same priorities and focus as in the past. Firms may well wish to consider whether the move towards 'one-to-one' relationships with customers actually requires a marketing *department* at all. In this situation it may be preferable instead to develop the attitude of mind known as a *marketing orientation* throughout the organisation, whereby employees at all levels are charged with prioritising the meeting of customer needs. This contention is supported by Piercy (1997), who notes that the current emphasis upon the value of cross-functional teams conducting 'pan-company marketing' may obviate the need for marketing departments, especially if such project teams also cross organisational boundaries and blur the distinction between the internal and external environment.

This chapter concludes by looking to the future and considering whether the changes in the marketing function described here may provide a source of sustainable competitive advantage.

Conclusions

The recent well-publicised problems of the 'dot-coms' provide an opportunity for more traditional organisations to regain ground lost to new market entrants, as long as they can demonstrate the necessary (and ongoing) flexibility of structure described earlier in the chapter. In particular this means permitting the development of both intra- and inter-organisational networks upon which successful eBusiness strategies are increasingly dependent for the effective integration and dissemination of customer information. The chapter has also described examples of established organisations that have reached beyond the limitations of their traditional structures to generate useful synergies by combining elements of the 'online' and 'offline' in innovative ways. Herein perhaps lies a lesson for the much-maligned 'dot-coms', as well as the industry incumbents, in that a little flexibility of 'Internet-only' structures might now be somewhat overdue.

Acknowledgement

This chapter is based on work carried out under the European Community Targeted Social Economic Research (TSER) programme, project no. PL97–1084.

Notes

1 It is worth noting however, that some companies may have embraced the need for change *too* enthusiastically. One manager of a software company remarked: 'We start to get worried if change is not taking place every week even; the question is will we get left behind? We must change something. But often it's change for change's sake' (private conversation).
2 RS Component's strategy is based on the premise that: 'If *you* don't cannibalise your own customer base, then your competitors will be happy to do it for you' (private conversation, January 2000).
3 Indeed, at the time of writing it has been reported that Amazon is in talks with Wal-Mart about forming an alliance (*The Times Business*, 4 March 2001: 1). It is also worth noting here that even Lastminute.com has bowed to market trends and issued a paper-based Christmas 2000 catalogue.

References

Achrol, R.S. (1991) 'The evolution of the marketing organization: new focus for turbulent environments', *Journal of Marketing*, October: 77–93.

Anders, G. (2000) 'Power Partners', *Fast Company*, September, 146–58.

Aoki, A. (1984) *The Co-operative Game Theory of the Firm*, Oxford: Clarendon Press.

Burns, T. and Stalker, G.M. (1961) *The Management of Innovation*, London: Tavistock.

Coles, A.-M. and Harris, L. (2001) 'Testing goodwill: conflict and co-operation in new product development networks', *International Journal of Technology Management*, forthcoming.

Cope, N. (2000) 'No one hears you scream on the easy route to e-mail hell', *The Independent*, 14 August.

Day, G.S. (1998) 'Organising for interactivity', *Journal of Interactive Marketing*, 12, 1: 47–53.

DeBresson, C. and Amesse, F. (1991) 'Networks as innovators: a review and introduction to the issue', *Research Policy*, 20: 363–79.

Dickson, K., Coles, A.-M. and Lawton Smith, H. (1997) 'Staying the course: small firm strategies for long-term R&D collaboration', *Small Business and Enterprise Development Journal*, 4: 13–27.

Economist (1999) 'You'll never walk alone', *Survey: Business and the Internet*, 26 June: 71.

Freeman, R.E. (1997) 'A stakeholder theory of the modern corporation', in T. Beauchamp and N. Bowie (eds) *Ethical Theory and Business*, London: Prentice Hall, 66–76.

Hamel, G., Doz, Y. and Prahalad, C.K. (1989) 'Collaborate with your competitors—and win', *Harvard Business Review*, 67, 1: 133–9.

Hanson, W. (2000) *Principles of Internet Marketing*, Cincinnati: South-Western College Publishing.

Harris, L. (1999) 'Building inter-firm networks: a case study of EMC (SW) Ltd.', *International Journal of New Product Development and Innovation Management*, 1, 3: 211–18, September.

Jackson, P. and Harris, L. (2000) 'eBusiness and Organisational Change', paper presented to The eBusiness and eWork Conference, Madrid, October.

Kalakota, R. and Robinson, M. (1999) *e-Business: Roadmap for Success*, 2nd edn, Reading, MA: Addison Wesley.

Kleindl, B.A. (2001) *Strategic Electronic Marketing: Managing eBusiness*, Cincinnati: South-Western College Publishing.

Kumar, V. (1999) *Interactive Multimedia on the Internet*, Indianapolis: New Riders Publications.

McIntosh, M., Leipziger, D., Jones, K. and Coleman, G. (1998) *Corporate Citizenship: Successful Strategies for Responsible Companies*, London: Pitman Publishing.

Miles, R.E. and Snow, C.C. (1986) 'Network organisation: new concepts for new forms', *The McKinsey Quarterly*, Autumn.

Nadler, D. and Tushman, M. (1999) 'The organisation of the future: strategic imperatives and core competencies for the 21st century', *Organisational Dynamics*, 27: 45, July.

Piercy, N.F. (1997) *Market-Led Strategic Change*, 2nd edn, Oxford: Butterworth Heinemann.

Porter, M.E. (1980) *Competitive Strategy*, New York: Free Press.

Seth, J. and Sisodia, R. (1999) 'Re-visiting marketing's lawlike generalizations', *Journal of the Academy of Marketing Science*, 27, 1: 71–87.

Siegel, D. (2000) *Futurize Your Enterprise: Business Strategy in the Age of the E-customer*, New York: Wiley.

Stroud, D. (1998) *Internet Strategies: a corporate guide to exploiting the Internet*, Macmillan: Basingstoke.

Sunday Times, 10 Dec. 2000: 1 (Cohen, P. 'Amazon loses to offline rivals').

Symonds, M. (1999) 'The net imperative', *Survey: Business and the Internet*, *Economist*, 26 June.

Tapscott, D. (1995) *The Digital Economy*, New York: McGraw-Hill.

Tapscott, D., Ticoll, D. and Lowy, A. (2000) *Digital Capital*, London: Nicholas Brealey Publishing.

Turner, C. (2000) *The Information E-conomy*, London: Kogan Page.

van Rossum, W. and Hicks, E. (1996) 'Processes of Innovation: Combined insights from network and systems theory', paper presented at COST A3 Conference, Management of New Technology, Madrid.

Part 2

Workplace architecture and design

In Part 2 we turn to the realm of architecture and facilities management and examine their importance to the physical aspects of work. Chapter 4 by Cristina Caramelo Gomes, Ghassan Aouad and Marcus Ormerod focuses on 'sustainable workplace' design in the context of eBusiness and new methods of work. They note that a workplace is a central concept for several entities: the worker and his/her family, the employing organisation, the customers of the organisation, and the society as a whole. All have different expectations towards working methods and places, with the task of optimising the whole a daunting one. The work design phase is made more complex by new information and communication technologies, given the way they increase available design possibilities. At the same time, the authors argue, expectations of work and workplace conditions have grown because of the increased awareness of better options for performing work. The authors note that as part of these developments, workers themselves also need to adapt and that the new workforce needs much more flexibility than workers previously.

At the heart of the authors' argument is the belief that changes in work organisation must be designed in ways that sustain both social and ecological resources. To do this we need to overcome established practices in the design and building of workplaces, and support the greater temporal and spatial flexibility demanded in new methods of work. Indeed, by providing for new forms of occupancy (such as non-territorial offices and teleworking), they argue that we can both achieve a higher quality of working life and improve our relationships with the wider community.

The authors conclude by presenting a conceptual model to support the whole process of designing and managing a modern and flexible workplace. It therefore encapsulates their core argument that the new office should be a sustainable structure while also giving due consideration to environmental issues.

Chapter 5 by Martin van der Linden provides us with new insights into the interface between architecture and work design. The chapter provides a thorough analysis of basic concepts in architecture, such as context, construction and activities. It points out that the interaction between context and construction traditionally happened either in a sequential or, later, parallel space. Advances in communication, both at physical and information levels, have challenged these concepts with the introduction of the 'transitional space'.

This concept is particularly important to modern society and is analysed in some depth. Today, both organisations and people are in constant transitional spaces, either real or symbolic. As such, says van der Linden, 'construction is now actually creating the context' and not vice versa, as was the erstwhile case in architectural terms. This is not far from the metaphor of the Internet, where 'the medium becomes the message'. Both concepts show that in the modern information economy, basic hierarchical structures are deeply challenged.

In addition to analysis at a theoretical level, the chapter also offers insight on operational issues, such as room heights, usage of lifts, illumination, and the importance of proper air conditioning, to name just a few. An important message for property managers is that buildings must be built and accommodated for constant change; as such—and to echo the previous authors—*flexibility* has become a key concept in modern architecture. Van der Linden shows that as context and construct dissolve into one entity in transitional space, architecture and work design also seem to melt into one inseparable element.

4 The sustainable workplace and workplace design

Cristina Caramelo Gomes, Ghassan Aouad and Marcus Ormerod

Introduction

Cities have changed much over the last century, with many now boasting a population of more than 10 million people. This growth reflects a concentration of economic activities within a small geographical area. As part of this, we have seen a tremendous transformation in the nature of economies. The service, or tertiary, sector will clearly be the biggest work consumer in the next century (Gomes and Aouad 2000a). This fact has already changed the city's appearance over the last 30 years. The tertiary sector now occupies the core of the city (something that developments in eCommerce and eBusiness are likely to embed further). This, in turn, has led to mass commuter flows to and from the centres, with all the cost this incurs with regard to pollution, health, energy, urbanisation and social integration. Such commuter flows reflect the fact that the working habits and methods in services are very much the same as those employed since the industrial revolution. This unsustainable situation must change. As this chapter will explain, workplace designers and city planners need to find new and more sustainable ways of supporting economic processes.

The sustainable city implies a user-friendly environment. There are several issues here: the modus operandi of service businesses; the way individuals support themselves financially; how communities run their economic development; and how buildings and space are combined with new technologies to support new organisational designs and new methods of work. eBusiness developments provide a particularly interesting focus within this context. The new working practices they employ typically use new technologies to link people from different geographical locations and different areas of expertise. Developments in eBusiness thus have profound consequences for organisations.

Becoming an eBusiness means rethinking your organisation—large or small—to see where technology makes the difference. An eBusiness must have the willingness and desire to let technology improve every aspect of its business processes. This continual improvement and ability to adapt is part of what makes eBusiness so powerful and yet so daunting ... Because businesses are all different shapes and sizes, there is no single set of eBusiness technologies that is right for everyone. But in the end, almost all businesses come down to relationships. And that's what eBusiness is really about: It uses technology to build better relationships with customers, suppliers, and employees.

(Miller 2000)

But where do these relationships occur? The new methods of work suggest a new workplace culture which accepts that 'wherever one works is the workplace, be it a headquarters building, branch office, telework centre, home office, or an airplane, car, boat, airline club, restaurant, or hotel lobby' (Becker and Steele 1994: 113). Understanding that 'the workplace' depends on different locations and network communications is a crucial starting point for defining future requirements. A new set of assumptions is therefore needed. This might include, for instance, accepting that:

- Work happens all day long, wherever the person happens to be, in many different locations.
- Settings are tools to get things done, and as such are too expensive to use as status symbols.
- Workplaces that are well designed for their users will inherently project the right image.
- Appropriate choices by users result in better settings and stronger commitment to using them well.
- Space costs should be controlled without compromising the best achievement of overall objectives.

(Becker 1994)

Despite these assumptions it is important to recognise that workplaces involve individuals with different sets of requirements and preferences, depending on their activities and personalities. Here, the office provides the physical support that in turn supplies four basic business functions: 'a place where individuals develop their activities, a system infrastructure, a cultural interchange and a financial opportunity' (Worthington 1997: 41). More than just an asset to the company, the workplace building is a crucial resource in the performance of activities and relations between human beings. The way space influences work activity—as well professional and social relations—raises important psychological and sociological issues. Here we can consider the user as a:

Social Being who needs to communicate with other human beings;
Physical Being who interacts with the physical things surrounding him or her;
Mental Being who is influenced by space and communication;
Aesthetic Being who appreciates things of beauty;
Pragmatic Being who requires some functionality and rationalism in a space;
Ethical Being who seeks to reduce, recycle and reuse the working environment's waste.

The Sustainable Workplace should allow for a user-friendly environment and stimulate these relationships so that advantages are maximised and disadvantages minimised.

Aims, objectives and methodology

This chapter is based on the experience of the authors as architect, engineer and surveyor, with an interest in the impact of new methods of working on the planning of future physical workplaces and on the environment. Usually, the facilities where work takes place involve notorious inflexibility and inadaptability to new technology. The aim of this chapter is to identify the key parameters in reinventing the workplace. It brings together a review of the literature, and data from questionnaires and case studies. The literature review will enable us to discuss the state of the art in sustainability, workplaces, new methods of work, the psychology of the space, and the interaction between buildings and users. Questionnaires and case studies illustrate the empirical input and allow a comparison between experiences and the theoretical model presented at the end of the chapter.

Background/historical perspective of office planning

The planning process for a building is usually based on the cost of the square metre, implanted in a well-defined location where the 'image' may be the main issue, with matters of functionality and environmental degradation being disregarded or neglected. This sort of approach typically leads to problems of 'sick building syndrome', poor support for the users (as well as for their personal relationships within building), and eventually to rapid building obsolescence.

Research about work environments undertaken in the last few decades illustrates the diversity of approaches to workplace design. They cover a number of disciplines, including architecture, ergonomics, design, work sociology, social psychology and environmental psychology (Fisher 1989), all of which have an important contribution to make towards better planning, management and occupancy of workplaces.

Approaches to office design at the beginning of the 1950s were very similar to those to factory design. The standard production workplace, rooted as it was in industrial organisation, reflected a need for personalisation, identification and health issues. In the 1960s much of Europe adopted the cellular office, one that was 'narrow in depth and cellular in plan, with small offices served off a central corridor' (Worthington 1997: 28). The USA introduced the 'open space' concept. Both were made possible by air-conditioning and fluorescent lighting. Subsequent European innovations included the 'landscape office', which produced an office of casual meeting places, coffee bars, and generous space for each worker in the open space plan, with private enclosed offices for the managers. The criticism of the 1970s was supported by the emergence of the tension created between corporate and individual aspirations. There was need for a workplace that permitted communication between users and space for teamwork, as well for spaces that allowed identification with personal areas. The 1980s saw the innovation of networked computers, which then began to proliferate on office desks. The consequences of this continue to drive innovation in office use and design (Worthington 1997: 31). However, whereas in the UK and North America this led to the production of large buildings, as simple and cheap as possible, northern Europe developed the concept of the 'combi office', where the shared space lived together with personal enclosure. These examples developed three types of layouts: highly cellular, combi-office, and group rooms.

The recession at the end of the 1980s and 1990s led to the development of office real estate, in Europe as in USA. The result was the standardisation of office buildings without a specific function or user. As Worthington observed:

> A double shift has therefore occurred in the expectations of what buildings should offer end users: on the one hand the developers are forced to pay more respect to the complex, varied and changing needs of end users; on the other hand, the end users are demanding buildings and offices environments that can both add value to the ways they want to work but in ways that minimise their costs.
>
> (Worthington 1997: 37).

The consequence of this is that many buildings reflect the objectives and economic power of the firm and minimise or misunderstand the space and environmental needs of the users and the tasks they perform.

Sustainable development

Sustainability has become a very important issue over the past few decades, as reflected in writing on the subject. These efforts have not generally changed the understanding of the ordinary person about the concept of sustainability, however: the majority of people still relate it to environmental practices alone and evaluate it on a short-term basis. This approach also leads to a negative appraisal of the concept's implementation, as short-term cost are often high. There are also other economic and technical difficulties in implementing the concept on a wide scale, of course.

Individuals and profit-driven organisations often base their cost-benefit analysis on a short-term return. As such, there is little incentive for them to pursue a sustainable approach in their activities. Incentives to do otherwise could include policy measures to reduce the initial investment, thus cutting distance to the break-even point, or measures to punish operators working in a non-sustainable way. The important issue, whatever the solution may be, is its *effectiveness*. If the way forward is to be positive measures, such as those intended to reduce the initial overhead, it is essential that they actually reduce it. If the penalty scheme is used instead, then penalties must be set in such a way, and to such an extent, that its effectiveness is not put at risk. In fact, if the penalties are not heavy enough, or not strictly enforced, it may prove to be more cost effective not to shift to more sustainable methods of work.

Metropolitan areas, it can be argued, are unsustainable. Natural resources are wasted, peripheries are economically dependent on the central cities, and rural areas are being deserted (Booth 1998). Even today, the features of the Industrial Revolution orientate working methods in the various economic sectors. Industry continues to pollute the rivers, lakes and seas; the use of paper is still commonplace; and individuals are still commuting despite the possibilities offered by the new technologies.

A more sustainable view of economic development is set out by the World Commission on Environment and Development (the Brundtland Commission 1987) in its report *Our Common Future*:

> Sustainable development is development that meets the needs of the present without compromising the ability of future generations to meet their own needs.

It contains within it two key concepts:

> . . . the concept of *needs*, in particular the essential needs of the world's poor, to which overriding priority should be given; and the idea of limitations imposed by the state of technology and social organisation on the environment's ability to meet present and future needs.
>
> (Brundtland Commission 1987: 35)

Many actions are required to fulfil this goal. The report notes that living sustainably depends on accepting a duty to seek harmony with other people and with nature. This, in turn, means adopting life styles and development paths that respect and work within nature's limits. It can be done without rejecting the many benefits that modern technology has brought, provided that technology also works within those limits.

This section aims to provide an overview of sustainability topics, in order to acquaint the reader with the sections that follow. These range in scale from global sustainability to the sustainable workplace: business strategy, sustainable livelihoods, sustainable buildings and, finally, sustainable workplaces.

Business principles for a sustainable and competitive future

Business as usual is no longer an option—for government, the private sector or for individual citizens. Our soil, waters, forests and minerals are not inexhaustible. Farms, industries, homes and lifestyles must become more sustainable in every community on our planet. To be sustainable, development must improve economic efficiency, protect and restore ecological systems, and enhance the well-being of all peoples (International Institute for Sustainable Development 2000).

The twentieth century brought huge transformations in people's way of life. Cities have grown up whose main function is 'employment', surrounded by peripheries that incorporate housing. These features have spread with the proliferation of the tertiary sector. The clear demarcation between working and housing requires massive commuter movements, most of them in private transportation. This causes time-wasting, parking difficulties, an increase in air pollution, stress, and poor quality of life. Traditional methods of work as a whole are characterised by issues of unsustainability related not only to the environment but also to society.

The company of the twenty-first century will need to assume and implement 'sustainable development' as a key point to its activities. In so doing, sustainability will be more an economic issue than just an environmental one. Every new project, service or product will need to be evaluated according to sustainable principles. The objective will be to control and/or minimise any negative consequences. Companies will need to apply the principle of life-cycle management in order to appraise each stage of its activity: this covers the full spectrum, from research and development, recycling and reuse process, and the production process, through to transportation and distribution, sales and customer use, and ultimate disposal. Employees' behaviour will demand continuous training, survey and assessment. Companies will need to be aware of any applicable environmental law, or go beyond that by creating its own regulations.

Business Charter for sustainable development

The International Chamber of Commerce formulated a Charter of principles for sustainable development. In it they point out that there should be a common goal, and not a conflict, between economic development and environmental protection (International Chamber of Commerce 1991). The Charter outlines a number of key principles, these include *corporate priority*, which urges businesses to recognise environmental management as among the highest corporate priorities, and *integrated management*, which calls on businesses to integrate fully policies, programmes and practices on sustainability, and as an essential element of management in all its functions. Of particular relevance to workplace redesign are principles related to *facilities and operations*. Here, the Charter calls on enterprises to develop, design and operate facilities, and conduct activities, that take into consideration the efficient use of energy and materials, the sustainable use of renewable resources, the minimisation of adverse environmental impact and waste generation, and the safe and responsible disposal of residual wastes.

Sustainable livelihoods

In addition to the above, we also need a broader vision of how people can meet their needs in a sustainable way. Attempting to solve the world's employment crisis using conventional job creation through sustained economic growth cannot work (North American Regional Consultation on Sustainable Livelihoods 1995). Sustainable livelihood policies aim to provide meaningful work that fulfils the social, economical, cultural and spiritual needs of all members of a community. They promote production based on renewable energy and the regeneration of local resource endowments. They also utilise technology that is ecologically fitting, socially just and humane, and which enhances, rather than displaces, community knowledge and skills. Sustainable livelihood policies also aim to reduce, as much as possible, travel to the workplace and the distance between producers and users (North American Regional Consultation on Sustainable Livelihoods 1995).

These items comprise a set of principles for holistic arrangements, and underline the need for participation in decision making. They call attention to the quality and innovative character of work, and categorise needs over demands.

Green buildings

According to Cohen-Rosenthal *et al.* (2000), many technologies are already available that would allow a transformation towards green buildings (that is, those facilities which use energy efficiently and are renewable where feasible). Yet much remains to be done to make this standard practice. They argue for public policy to take a leading role in promoting such transformation. This could include, they suggest, building codes, expanded R&D, education and training, and financial incentives, all of which could further the public interest in green buildings and jump-start the market. They warn, however, that we will only achieve market transformation through a constructive and cooperative dialogue between the construction industry, government agencies, occupants and owners, and other stakeholders.

Even today, at the turn of the millennium, many professionals do not evaluate the life cycle of building objects. New materials are usually applied, along with heavy and rigid building structures. Sick building syndrome is still widespread, although often not identified. A green building should, by contrast, use renewable energy and natural resources; have a user-friendly environment; promote occupant health and safety; and be flexible enough to support the changes that the future can bring. Such criteria can be met by attending to a number of areas. For example, the IISDnet Principles for Sustainable Development identify a number of items to be considered in building design and construction. BuildingGreen 2000 has elaborated a checklist for Environmentally Responsible Design and Construction (BuildingGreen 1995; see Table 4.1 for more details).

Sustainable workplaces

A sustainable workplace takes into account the *ecological* and *social* consequences of operations, as well as economic ones. The sustainable workplace is a broad subject. It embraces: features of the community where the business takes place; business organisation and its impact in the community; characteristics of the building where people work; equipment, furnishings and finishing of the physical place; the interaction between people within the workplace; and interactions with the environment.

Traditional workplaces (see Figure 4.1) raise problems related to health, security, poor productivity, deficient communication, and a bad fit between private and professional life. According to TCO (2000), Western societies have relied too much on non-renewable resources. As a consequence, the natural environment is deteriorating, while a majority of the population has become accustomed to excessive consumption. TCO also adds that, while many societies have high levels of unemployment, a growing number of people burn out because of high time-pressure and heavy workload.

One major constraint on overcoming this is the fear of the change. A traditional mentality was built over a century or so, which will take time to become adapted to the new realities. This mentality is linked to the use of natural

Table 4.1 Checklist for environmentally responsible design and construction

Design	Siting and land use	Materials	Equipment	Job site and business
Smaller is better	Renovate older buildings	Avoid ozone-depleting chemicals in mechanical equipment and insulation	Install high-efficiency heating and cooling equipment	Protect trees and topsoil during site work
Design an energy-efficient building	Create community	Use durable products and materials	Install high-efficiency lights and appliances	Avoid use of pesticides and other chemicals that may leach into the groundwater
Design buildings to use renewable energy	Encourage in-fill and mixed-use development	Choose low-maintenance building materials	Install water-efficient equipment	Minimise job-site waste
Optimise material use	Minimise automobile dependence	Choose building materials with low embodied energy	Install mechanical ventilation equipment	Make your business operations more environment-ally responsible
Design water-efficient, low-maintenance landscaping	Value site resources	Buy locally produced building materials		Make education a part of your daily practice
Make it easy for occupants to recycle waste	Locate buildings to minimise environmental impact	Use building products made from recycled materials		
Look into the feasibility of graywater	Provide responsible on-site water management	Use salvaged building materials when possible		
Design for durability	Situate buildings to benefit from existing vegetation	Seek responsible wood supplies		
Design for future reuse and adaptability		Avoid materials that will offgas pollutants		
Avoid potential health hazards: radon, mould, pesticides		Minimise use of pressure-treated lumber		
		Minimise packaging waste		

Source: inspired by BuildingGreen 1995.

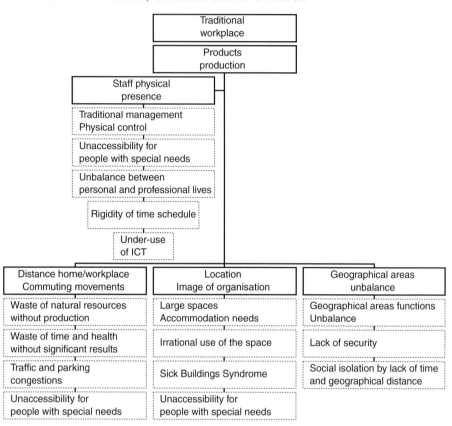

Figure 4.1 Traditional workplace characteristics

resources and involves considerable ignorance concerning the possibilities offered by technical developments in the recycling of materials. Different approaches are also needed in planning. The majority of tertiary organisations are small, private companies, aimed at short and medium-term profits. Public organisations, on the other hand, are often characterised by heavy structures with little cost control. Together with a lack of awareness as to what new technologies can offer in terms of more sustainable management, this leads to many missed opportunities.

As the present situation becomes more unsustainable, it is therefore essential to identify incentives and practices to promote change. Uppermost here are the features of a sustainable workplace (see Figure 4.2). Commitment to such features by all stakeholders in workplace design is clearly important, something that will require appropriate systems of participation, training and assessment. The authors have considered two case studies that illustrate the concept of the sustainable workplace.

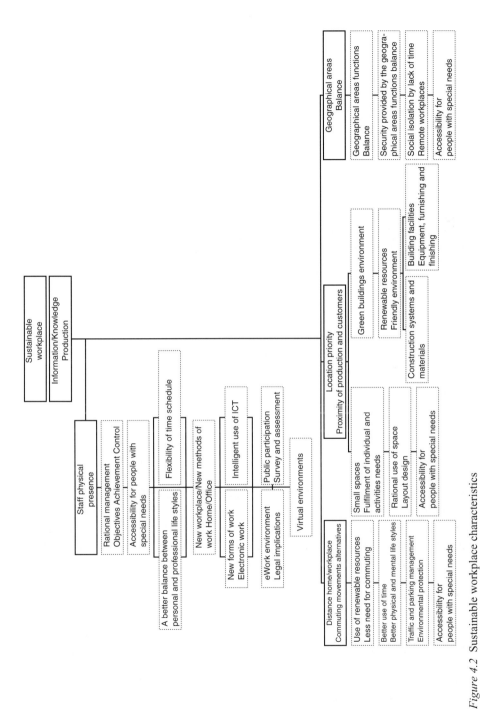

Figure 4.2 Sustainable workplace characteristics

Totta Ogander, from the environmental office at Sanga-Saby, described how a run-down conference centre has become popular and profitable by placing a strong emphasis on environmental issues. Employees were provided with information on the financial situation of the conference centre, and also received environmental education. Members of staff were involved in improving and developing their workplace on an ongoing basis. The environmental aspects of Sanga-Saby included: using renewable energy (including renewable energy vehicles); use of lake water, ecological food products and long-lasting inventory items; using few chemicals; limiting air and water pollution; and sorting waste to reduce the weight of waste per guest. Personnel at Sanga-Saby have even followed the public waste transport to make sure, once sorted, that the waste is handled properly by the authorities.

A different approach to achieving a sustainable workplace was described by Ola Lohman, who was responsible for the concept of sustainable development at KPA, an asset management fund and pension insurance company owned by local and city councils in Sweden. Ola Lohman stressed the importance of defining what you wish to achieve in order to make it happen. His definition of sustainability is based on Agenda 21 and the triple bottom line of its ecological, social and economic aspects. The aim of KPA was to work for a better future for both people and the environment. Lohman stressed the importance of 'measuring' sustainability. As such, KPA was introducing audits on its ecological and social results as a complement to the mandatory financial audits (TCO 2000).

Once the strategic issues are solved, it is important how one considers the internal issues. The organisation can be laid out to provide hierarchical areas, function areas, team/concentrative areas, each one with its own needs and requirements. Ergonomics, and the movement for quality of working life—together with the socio-technical approach to organisational design—recently converged in their focus on these matters. This moved attention towards this satisfaction of workers' full professional, emotional, social, self and cognitive expression in respect of their physical integrity (Butera 1995; Mariani 1997).

Ergonomics therefore still plays an important role in the analysis, design and quality of work. But cultural, kinaesthesia and proximity issues are also flagged as being important for a sustainable, user-friendly environment. And while the identification of the individual with the workplace remains important, we must remember here that this commitment should not contradict his/her personal lifestyle choices.

New methods of work: concepts and interactions

One common new method of work involves working in a remote location, connected to the employer or customers by information technology (IT). The idea is not new, of course; in fact, for many years some companies, even industrial ones, have been using what we might call 'long distance work' (work performed by an individual for an employer outside its office or plant). Consider overseas media and local correspondents, female manufacturers working at home, and many other examples. The big difference is IT—technology that captures, transmits, processes, stores and retrieves information (Reid 1994). IT has expanded work possibilities, allowing many new tasks to be performed away from the employer's site. 'Telecommuting', as this is often referred to, is thus a work option that reduces dependency on transportation by increasing dependency on IT, and can often be accomplished with 'no more exotic a technology than a telephone' (Nilles 1998).

A related concept, 'telecooperation', is the use of electronic networks to develop and sustain work relationships. This can occur at a local level (village, town or city) or at a national level—or regionally or globally. Allied to this are developments in 'teletrade', something particularly bound up with electronic commerce (business conducted through IT networks). Here, advanced IT, such as the Internet, is used to market and sell goods and services, to enhance customer relationships and to reach distant markets without the overhead of physical presence. The future is likely to show an increase in distance work, encompassing new, more flexible and decentralised forms of organisation, new opportunities for self-employment, and the downsizing of large firms with a trend towards the outsourcing of functions and activities (European Commission 1996).

New methods of work and eBusiness

New methods of work and related developments in eBusiness are not ends in themselves for companies, but rather the methods by which they achieve their goals. In the Information Society, to be effective and competitive, firms must identify the need for a continuous updating of strategies, training, information, techniques and tools appropriate to the new technology. The Internet and eBusiness are therefore having an enormous impact on organisations: they are affecting how organisations operate and how do they do business; they provide new opportunities for businesses of all sizes and have created a new sales channel. However, companies must be prepared to reorganise and restructure themselves continuously in order to realise these opportunities. This is because of the way eBusiness is affecting how people in organisations work together, share information and communicate with one another. It is also impacting on the transactions and connections that occur across the supply chain between suppliers, distributors and their customers (Jackson and Harris 2000).

Quality of life: family and personal commitments

The pressure exercised by the turbulent rhythm of the city is a major contributor to the reduction in the quality of life and the demise of the family structure. However, with the implementation of new methods of work we can expect certain improvements. It is important here to define what we mean by 'quality of life'. As a subject, it is something intimately connected with cultural issues and personal experiences, combining exterior influences and genetic ones. We can explore these factors by analysing new methods of work in terms of the Maslow pyramid, presented in Marlow (1999) (see Figure 4.3).

New methods of work can enhance employment, as well as the social integration of the individual. They may increase the number of jobs, thereby promoting the economic development of a residential zone, and may also provide for a greater security. Although some authors argue that new methods of working create or increase individual isolation, it is important to remember that, although the workplace can be considered as a meeting point, the pressure of urban life leaves little space for contacts outside work. We can argue, by contrast, that telework provides the opportunity to develop different contacts, improve social integration and give disabled people a chance to participate in community and professional life. These matters are important in strengthening the self-esteem of the individual, leading to greater self-realisation. This is not simply a question of survival but of personal accomplishment.

Workspace

The workplace has nowadays become the key site where professional and personal relationships emerge. From a Maslowian perspective, the individual

SELF-REALISATION

SELF-ESTEEM

INCLUDING MINORITIES

DYNAMIC URBAN LIFE/SECURITY

REDUCTION OF UNEMPLOYMENT LEVEL

Figure 4.3 Maslow/telework pyramid
Source: Gomes and Aouad (2000b)

searches in her/his professional life for the achievement of self-realisation. This is a journey through the stages of physiological survival, security, social integration and contact, self-esteem and finally self-actualisation. The workplace can support all of these phases, through work tasks themselves and through the environment where these take place. In fact, of course, the interaction of people engaged in new methods of work are always done with physical support: in other words, in *space*. How can this space provide for the achievement of individual/group self-realisation?

The successful planning of office space resides in the harmony of the triad presented by the requirements of the company, the users and the tasks to be performed. In the eBusiness era, these requirements are undergoing dynamic change. Telecommunications networks help overcome the constraints of geography, with knowledge workers interacting via IT with individuals and groups. Workplaces are thus increasingly geographically dispersed (to places which include the home).

Space, of course, is a determining factor of behaviour (Fisher 1989). Human beings, like other animals, have a territorial instinct: they react to the presence of another being and respond to the properties of the environment (Hall 1986). The workplace should therefore take care of issues concerning ergonomics, to provide a healthy and comfortable utilisation of facilities. In terms of social interaction, workspaces should also take account of issues of kinaesthesia and proximity (Becker and Steele 1994). These establish the required distance between people, with furniture arrangements playing a crucial role in supporting social spaces that allow for circulation and interaction.

The office of the 1990s

Nowadays, the physical place of the company is changing in size, dimension, features and location. Crucial to these changes has been the contribution of network communications, including road and train networks, as well as IT. However, the design of office buildings has often failed to meet the needs of the organisations that use them. The speculative nature of much office development has encouraged design focused on maximising economy and flexibility of space. In addition, even when a particular client has been directly involved, the design is often focused on corporate image expressed in reception spaces and façades. Finally, the very shape and design of the office building has been heavily restricted by planning legislation. The introduction of new technologies in the office has changed the expectations of users relating to new processes and tasks. The idea of an individual workplace within the office, or of one seat per person, has been challenged (Worthington 1997).

While the new technologies have provided new work possibilities, realising these must take careful consideration of how individual and team areas are created, with the main objective being to support social contact between individuals. The concepts involved in the new ways of working—which are premised on the exploitation of new technology and encourage work to be carried out when and where it is most suitable—have been combined with ideas about simplification that permit flexibility and cost control (Eley and Marmot 1995). As Eley points out, these principles are reflected in a number of common terms used today in space planning: for example: 'quiet rooms', 'war rooms', 'project rooms', 'team areas', 'group bases', 'work lounges' and so on. All apply to spaces used by people for different tasks at different times and in different combinations.

The changing conception of the workplace

In the twenty-first century, the human resources of an organisation are seen as evermore important.

As we have seen, the effective use of human resources raises important questions with respect to the design of the workplace. Important contributions to discussions can be made here through Becker's concept of organisational 'ecology'.

> The characteristic that most distinguishes organisational ecology from the more traditional disciplines of organisational behaviour (including human resources, organisational development, human factors, architecture and engineering, and industrial engineering) is concern for the *total workplace*; this concern draws on all these disciplines but is broader in its scope than any one of them individually.
>
> (Becker and Steele 1994: 13)

More than the workstation where the work is carried out, the total workplace includes all the facilities that influence the performance of employees. This includes meeting rooms, cafeteria, parking, fitness and nursery facilities. The fact is that the majority of companies employ a traditional approach to workplace design and management, based on economic and location considerations, with a general ignorance of users' needs.

The search for more effective and competitive performance may lead to the support of remote forms of work, where individuals are supported in their activities outside the main office facility. Such moves may have a significant impact on the broader scale, of course, and affect region, community and housing developments. But while remote working calls on us to rethink the role of office facilities, other questions are raised. Workplaces also need to support different timetables, and cope with high-density periods of work. They should be capable of supporting and increasing communication between individuals, leading to better relationships between employees, customers and the community in general.

Non-territorial offices

The above developments are commonly bound up with talk of so-called 'non-territorial offices'. As Becker explains:

> Whether called hoteling, non-territorial, just-in-time, free address, group address, or shared office, the essence of the unassigned office approach is the same: the individual employee has no dedicated personally assigned office, workstation, or desk.
>
> (Becker and Steele 1994: 117)

Such notions also reflect accounts of the 'virtual office'. According to Eley and Marmot (1995), this relies on the idea that technology can route communications effectively so that people can be seamlessly connected, no matter where they are. As such, he says, the old certainty of location is effectively replaced by the new certainty of reaching you, as 'your office is where you are'.

The notion that 'work is where the worker is working' raises questions about communicating the results of work and being reachable by colleagues, supervisors and clients. There are several solutions here, and concern mobile and fixed telephone communications and the place where the core of business takes place. Telephone and electronic communications therefore have a crucial importance. Network collaboration applications, also called groupware or teamware, are also crucial, particularly where interaction across time and space is needed.

Although remote work solutions are likely to be crucial to developments in eBusiness, the new office—be it a non-territorial office or otherwise—will still maintain an important role in the design of work, although with different requirements and functions. The new workplace may therefore not have personal places or workstations, or even places with an exclusive function. *Flexibility* is thus the rule, with space easily updated to new functions, equipment and individuals. The new workplace may even be more like the 'club', where people meet in order to define strategies, present results and integrate themselves into a team. Investment in space and equipment is therefore needed in a way that allows or encourages communication between individuals. Worthington sums the situation up nicely:

> Personal interaction or cultural interchange forms a large element of office activity. How people interact is changing, influenced by technology and by

the needs of individuals. The building needs to provide an environment that is conducive to improving all forms of communication and interchange, from face-to-face meetings to video conferencing. Employees are increasingly demanding a work environment that allows for more informal interaction so the building will need to provide informal meeting space and social amenities.

(Worthington 1997: 42)

Conceptual model

This chapter has highlighted the fact that in planning office designs which are both desirable and effective, data regarding a number of factors must be collected: company aims, the requirements of new methods of work (NMW), and the preferences and needs of the users who work there. Each one has its own objectives, with office space becoming the physical stage where they are performed, either positively or negatively. From this it is possible to define a set of requirements for each of the parts involved (see Table 4.2), which in turn feeds into a conceptual model (see Figure 4.4):

The model is supported by the survey of each of the parts involved and is developed in a continuous and cyclical process of survey and data collection—a process that reflects the dynamic and constant changes of new methods of work as people expectations change. The model underlines the point that the new office should be designed as a sustainable structure, giving due consideration to environmental issues in both its construction and post-

Table 4.2 Data for the conceptual model

Companies	NMW	Users	Space
Reduce space occupancy overheads	Decentralised forms of work	Territory—identification with the company as the space environment	Functionality and rationality for task performance
Improve productivity—be creative	IT and ICT requirements	Privacy for group interactions	Comfort issues such as light, sound/noise, temperature, moisture, as well as finishing and furniture
Effectiveness	Continuous learning process	Physical and social needs	Status and territory of each work-individual. Kinaesthesia and proximity considerations.
Competitiveness	Skilled workforce	Office as an extension of the house, workplace as an extension of the body	Layout with different possibilities of activities and communications performance
Growth	Remote work environments	Feel at home	Capability of continuous change

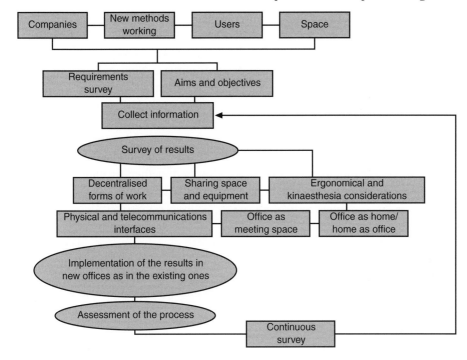

Figure 4.4 Conceptual model

occupancy maintenance. The workspace, given its layout, should guarantee the capacity to cope with the changes that time and innovations are certain to bring. The spatial layout, and its influence on human behaviour, will entail continuous assessment in order to supply the privacy, identity and communication desired. The implementation of the model should also attend to cultural changes and shifts in modes of interaction at individual, company and geographical levels.

Conclusions

This chapter has shown that the twentieth century approach to economic development has proved unsustainable. Natural resources have been wasted, pollution is now a major problem and inequity between regions and individuals is tremendous. Government policies have proved to be ineffective against the sustainability problem. However, it has been argued that sustainable development can improve economic efficiency on a long-term basis, protect and restore ecological systems, and enhance the well being of all people.

As the Information Society and related developments in eCommerce and eBusiness unfold, there are therefore many challenges in designing workplaces and methods that meet social, economic and ecological needs. These include, for instance, the economic development of communities and the integration of the individual into a user-friendly work environment. New methods of work and eBusiness structures are therefore not ends in themselves but the means by which we achieve sustainable environment. The workplace is more than the property asset of a company. It provides the physical and social context that shapes and supports the behaviour of the users towards a range of changing aims. Agents in office planning, from workplace designer to the post-occupancy managers, should therefore work closely together to understand and manage change, and thereby meet these aims in a sustainable way.

References

Bagnara, S., Mariani, M. and Parlangeli, O. (1999) 'Quality of working life in services', in *Working Life in the Information Society*: http://www.niwl.se/nl2000/workshops/workshop24/report_en.asp [Accessed 30 October 2000].

Becker, F. and Steele, F. (1994) *Workplace by Design*, San Francisco: Jossey-Bass.

Booth, D. (1998) *The Environmental Consequences of Growth*, London: Routledge.

Brundtland Commission (1987) *Our Common Future*, Oxford: Oxford University Press.

BuildingGreen, Inc (1995) 'Establishing priorities with green building', *Environmental Building News*, 5, 4 September/October, http://www.buildinggreen.com/features/4–5/priorities.html [Accessed 30 October 2000].

Butera, F. (1995) quoted in Bagnara *et al.* (1999).

Cohen-Rosenthal, E., Schlarb, M. and Thorne, J. (2000) *Build It Right: Cleaner Energy For Better Buildings*, Renewable Energy Policy Project, 10, March http://www.repp.org [Accessed 24 October 2000].

Eley, J. and Marmot A. (1995) *Understanding Offices*, London: Penguin Books.

European Commission (1996) *Green Paper—Living and Working in the Information Society: People First*, High Level Expert Group, COM (96) 339, final.

Fisher, G.N. (1989) *Psychologie des Espaces de Travail*, Paris: Armand Colin.

Gomes, C. and Aouad, G. (2000a) 'Telework, housing and urban plan', in *Proceedings of the Sixth European Assembly on Telework and New Methods of Work—Telework '99*, 22–24 September 1999, Aarhus, Bruxelles: EU: 139–54.

—— (2000b) 'New methods of working', in *Proceedings of Bizarre Fruit 2000, National Conference of Postgraduate Research in the Built and Human Environment*, 9–10 March, 321–36, University of Salford.

Hall, E.T. (1986) *A Dimensão Oculta*, Lisboa: Relogio D'Agua.

International Chamber of Commerce (1991) *Business Charter for Sustainable Development*, http://www.iccwbo.org [Accessed 30 October 2000].

International Institute for Sustainable Development (2000) *Moving from Principles to Practice*, http://iisd.ca/business [Accessed 3 November 2000].

Jackson, P. and Harris, L. (2000) 'eBusiness and organizational change', in B. Sanford-Smith and Paul T. Kidd (eds) *E-Business: Key Issues, Applications Technologies*, Oxford: IOS Press.

Mariani, M. (1997) quoted in Bagnara *et al.* (1999).

Maslow, A.H. (1999) *Towards a Psychology of Being*, 3rd edn, New York: Wiley.

Miller, M.J. (ed.) (2000), 'Building e-Business relationships', *PC Magazine*, http://www.zdnet.com/pcmag/stories/reviews/0,6755,2591235,00.html [Accessed 24 October 2000].

Nilles J. (1998) *Transportation Research* 22A, 4: 301–17.

North American Regional Consultation on Sustainable Livelihoods (1995) *Principles of Sustainable Livelihoods*, http://iisd1.iisd.ca/pcdf/1995/princsl.html [Accessed 3 November 2000].

TCO (2000) *Report from Workshop on the Sustainable Workplace*, http://www.niwl.se/wl2000/workshops/workshop51/article_en.asp [Accessed 3 November 2000].

5   Transition!

The transformation of the design and use of corporate architecture

Martin van der Linden

Introduction

Architects, facility managers and corporate real estate agents must regularly wake up in a cold sweat at night. More and more businessmen and women rely heavily, sometimes solely, on information-gathering and communications technology, such as laptops and mobile phones, to support their business activities. The increasing mobility of these appliances gives them the opportunity to spend more time 'on the job', which is increasingly outside the conventional office. This migration and mobility of the work force must cause apprehension, if not sheer anxiety, to those professionals whose very existence depends on developing, designing and maintaining corporate office buildings. It is almost trivial to state that technological developments are moving at Internet speed. The well known principle of change in the computer industry called Moore's law, laid down by Gordon Moore, co-founder of Intel, states that the capacity of semiconductors will double every 18 months and that the price of computing power will halve every 18 months. Facing this kind of reality, many real-estate related professionals, are left perplexed and confused—or they simply try to ignore what is happening. Change is the buzzword of the eBusiness environment; and architecture, or the very act of building, seems to be an acronym of change.

At a certain point in time, and that can be in a not too distant future, will we look back and only vaguely remember these archaic entities called offices? Will the ever-growing eBusiness environment make the building of offices obsolete or marginal? If so, what will replace them?

This chapter will do two things: it will try to capture the essence of the conceptual moves in the development of the office (or, more specifically, the office building) in order to understand its impact on today's eBusiness. Second, although this study is not merely intended as a historical analysis, it will try to reconstruct the development of the office through time, in order to find ways of anticipating the new and ever changing role of the design of spaces where corporate work can take place.

Setting the framework

The office—corporate architecture—developed within the framework of the system of industrialisation. The changes that have been (and are) taking place in the working environment all relate to this process of industrialisation and to the four variables of work: the workforce, the organisation, technology and space. These variables are all linked to the distinct changes in the system of industrialisation. In the first two phases the emphasis of the working environment was on the variable 'space'. Today the prominence of space as the place in which to work is changing, and this is having a significant impact on the definition of the office, of corporate architecture.

Situating the change

Analysis of the three subsystems in architecture: a systematic approach

A systematic approach to architecture defines architecture as the development of a process, more specifically a design construction process, in which ideas, in architectural terms called 'the programme', are realised.

A process forms a system. A system is constituted by elements and these elements of the system are related—if not they would simply be called a loose collection of elements. The relationships between the elements are of primary interest here. A relationship can be said to exist between element A and element B if they influence each other. These relationships form a hierarchical structure, an order (Gordon 1978: 1; Saaty and Kearns 1984: 12; Flood and Carson 1988: 7). We can distinguish, in the process of construction that leads to architecture, three distinct groups of elements that form three subsystems, clear systems with initially an apparent boundary. (Later we will see that the boundaries become less apparent.) Identifying the relationships between the elements of the subsystems helps to identify the boundaries and delimit the systems.

The three subsystems in architecture are: the context (the immediate surrounding, the site), the construction (the act of building and the materials used) and the activities (the translation of the programme, the use of the building). All these subsystems have elements; these elements, in turn, have components, and the components, attributes. An element of a building is, for example, its furniture, a component of furniture, a chair or a table; an attribute of the chair is its colour, texture, size or shape.

Our main interest will be the interrelationships between the subsystems, their changing hierarchy, extending boundaries and their limits. In order to see these changes we will first briefly investigate what the three subsystems consist of.

The context

The context of a building means the immediate setting, the surrounding site, the location. But we can also talk about a cultural, economical, social, structural or historical context. Context etymologically (Latin: contextus) means a joining-together and suggests a relation to the surrounding: con-text interweaving.

Construction

The process of construction is the art of elements ordered—ordered in such a way that together they form a structure of what we call architecture. The elements for construction are taken from the context. Initially the elements are taken directly and in their pure form from the immediate surrounding. As such there exists a clear relationship between the process of construction and the context (see Figure 5.1).

The context limits, as the elements used for construction are limited. We only have to think of igloos built in the Arctic, where ice, because of the harsh Northern conditions, is the only element available for construction. Thus, the specific climatic and geographic situations of the context are the limits.

Activities

The context limits not only the process of construction, but the activities as well. The most dominating limitation on earth is the fact that a day is divided

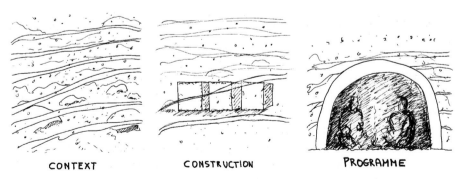

CONTEXT   CONSTRUCTION   PROGRAMME

Figure 5.1 The three subsystems of architecture: context, construction and programme (Drawing by the author)

into an approximately even amount of time of daylight and darkness. Humans, being physically equipped to perform their activities during the day, created a new time context when they invented fire to continue their actions at night and extended the limit of the context (O'Dea 1958: 223).

This is what is happening to the three subsystems in architecture: a constant shifting of borders and limits. We can distinguish three major phases in the hierarchical relationships of the three subsystems that created three distinct architectural spaces. We will briefly describe two of these spaces: sequential and parallel space. The third type, transitional space, will be discussed in more detail later.

Sequential space

First, in an agricultural society the context is the dominating subsystem; it restricts the process of construction and severely limits the activities. I would like to call this kind of space 'sequential'. Sequential means that there is some kind of repetition, such as the changing of seasons, that dominates the carrying out of activities that are dependent on the seasonal cycle. It is the sequential nature of time that is at the base of local identity.

Parallel space

As we saw before, the invention of the use of fire was the first, and arguably the most important, step towards shifting the weight from context to activity— the start of the process of modernisation. By slowly freeing the process of construction from the context (something that happened thousands of years ago and accelerated in the last couple of hundred years), a shift takes place where the balance between the three subsystems changes. Instead of having a dominant context, the process of construction (or the process of industrialisation, as the process is not limited to architecture) will become prominent. Construction allows for a contextual freedom, a freedom that increases constantly. This is the second form of architectural space that I would like to call a 'parallel' space, as there remains a strong relationship, a feedback between the sequential and the parallel space. This feedback is what Marshall Berman calls 'the strange dialectical dance' of modernisation (Berman 1988: 90). Modernism is the very expression of the process of modernisation and is both an expression of, and a reaction against, this very process. As a result, this void, this schism of against and for, is omnipresent in the modern world. The limit of the context however was, in combination with the sequential character of the activities, what created the very identity of place. Most modern writers (and architects) struggle with this inherent duality of modernism. The struggle can be clearly seen in the writings and buildings of Le Corbusier. In 1923 he hails industrialisation, envisioning his dream of a house like a machine, a mass-produced dwelling that would be 'beautiful in the same way that the tools and instruments which accompany our existence are beautiful' (quoted in Frampton 1987: 153). Twelve years later he abandoned this purist view (which he never could realise to its full extent anyway) and emphasised the importance of the use of local materials in order for his buildings to take a vernacular form (Frampton 1987: 153).

The changes that altered the shape of corporate architecture

We can see that a transition similar to that of a sequential space into a parallel space appeared in the design of the workplace. In the development of the office as we know it today, the emphasis has, for the last 200 years or so, remained on the variable space (*The Economist* 1995: 89). This move is part of the progress that strives, as we saw before, of reducing the time-space of the process of modernisation.

A systematic or, better, cybernetic approach towards a description of work, identifies four variables of work: the workforce, the organisation and administration of work, the technology, and the workspace (see Figure 5.2). The interrelationship of these four variables has for thousands of years remained more or less unchanged. What has been, and still is changing, however, is the emphasis on either one of these variables.

Organisation

According to Karl Wittfogel (Wittfogel 1957), the first major human developments, such as the irrigation works, called for the use of a systematic administration for the organisation and management of labour. In Egypt we can, for instance, see that scribes—the early office workers—took a privileged position within this strict and complex organisational hierarchy. Scribes were educated administrators and writing was a key to advancement in the government (Avrin 1991: 96). The workplace was as mobile as the technology used: the papyrus scroll (used for hundreds of years and later exported to many countries as an Egyptian monopoly), the reed pen, some seals, an eraser, and a writing tablet. Nothing would change for thousands of years (the Bank of England would use quill pens until as late as 1907 (Delegado 1979: 264)), as medieval clerks depended on basically the same technology (Bologna 1988: 22) and had a similar privileged, albeit more leisurely, position than the early scribes.

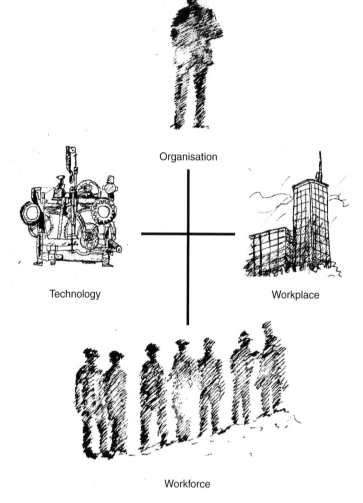

Figure 5.2 The four variable elements of work (Drawing by the author)

Modern organisation

It was not until after the industrial revolution, when the shift between context and production started to take on serious proportions, that the expanding administrative army would require large dedicated work environments. In Chicago, the astounding growth, from 300 people in 1833 to two million 70 years later, led to high urban densities and soaring land prices. This is turn gave rise to the first high-rise offices. The first skyscraper was built in New York. The Equitable Life Insurance Company Building constructed during

1868–70 was the first building with a dense office environment of commercial value. It contained three features which, according to Winston Weisman, when taken together in one building were the keywords of a skyscraper; height, passenger lifts and iron-framing (Weisman 1970: 129) (see Figure 5.3). From this moment on, a combination of inventions and increasing economic pressure become the basis of the new working environment. These inventions are all related to the space of the working environment.

Inventions

Bell's invention of the telephone in 1876 had an enormous impact on business as it reduced vast time-space distances to seconds. Messages, until the invention of the telephone, had to be delivered by hand and crucial business information would require waiting days, and sometimes, weeks for responses. In 1878 a switchboard was introduced in New Haven and the first automatic switchboard went into operation in 1892.

Elisha Graves Otis is often mistakenly attributed as being the inventor of the passenger lift. In fact he invented an automated safety device that prevented a lift from falling when a gear failed or a cable broke (Cowan 1978: 249). This invention was an important step towards the development of the skyscraper. In the Equitable Building the possibilities of the passenger lift were demonstrated for the first time. The Equitable, which was twice the height of an average office building, was an immediate financial success, as it demonstrated the value of the passenger lift (Weisman 1970: 125). Until the Equitable, the higher floors were reserved for lower clerks as they involved climbing many stairs. The new height in combination with the lift made the upper floors as rentable as the lower ones. This in turn made the expense of the tall structure feasible and increased the real estate value. The introduction of the lift and the fireproof skeletal frame by William LeBaron Jenny for the

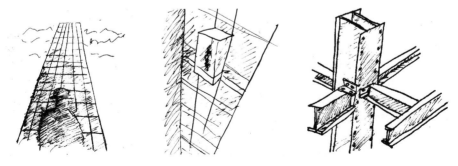

Figure 5.3 The elements of a true skyscraper according to Weisman: height, the passenger lift and a steel frame construction (Drawing by the author)

Home Office building in Chicago in 1883 doubled the height of office archi-tecture again (Travers 1994: 555) and had other consequences as well. The new construction technique would lead to structures where the load bearing would shift from the walls to the steel frame. Equally sized floor plans, designed around a service lift core, could now literally reach unlimited heights. Sullivan, a Chicago architect active from the 1890s, designed office buildings that were intentionally devoid of ornament, and both structurally and functionally dictated by these new demands of structure and function. Archi-tectural historian K. Frampton (1987) credits Sullivan with the invention of an architectural language appropriate to the high-rise frame. Sullivan devised an architectural vernacular where ornament 'should appear . . . [as if] it had come forth from the very substance of the material' (Frampton 1987: 55).

This tactic can be summarised in his 'form follows function', which has become a credo synonymous with the process of modernisation. Allan Delgado noted that inventions such as the typewriter, calculating machines and the mechanisation of postal despatch led to the departmentalisation of the office. Further, 'as work became more departmentalised and more people were involved, correspondence increased and an orderly filing system became essential' (Delegado 1997: 68). C. Wright noted in 1951 that 'each office within the skyscraper is a segment of the enormous file, part of the symbol factory that produces the billions of slips of paper that gear modern society into its daily shape' (Cortoda 1993: xvii). This might be taken as a summary of the office from the turn of the twentieth century until recently: the office as an orderly organised working environment, where each department, together with its files and clerks, are systematically accommodated.

Scientific Management and office space

The philosophy of Frederick Taylor, the father of Scientific Management, was in line with this notion of order and systematic maximisation to improve the efficiency of work. Taylor's method was to deskill the workforce through strict control and division of tasks. His ideas about the management of minimal costs and maximum efficiency are echoed in the office buildings of the turn of the last century. As land prices rose in New York and Chicago, the emphasis of work would go to the variable space, the working environment that was an expression of the same Scientific Management principles that, just as ruthlessly, controlled the clerks, no longer privileged, behind their typewrit-ers in the same way as workers in factories (Delgado 1979: 18). The new con-struction methods that now allowed an unlimited stacking of identical floor plans with electric lighting and air-conditioning, isolated the work force from its context in the same way that controlling the working environment could control the actual work itself. The office tower, filled with, as Nietzsche observed, 'state nomads (civil servants etc...) without home', both made and destroyed the city. Or, in Berman's words, 'the traditions of this city are distinctively modern, growing out of the city's existence as a symbol of modernity in the midst of a backward society' (Berman 1988: 285). In Manhattan, where Dutch architect Rem Koolhaas saw the rise of a city of 'blocks ... alone like an island, fundamentally on its own' (Koolhaas 1994: 97), the void would reach its peak to become something completely different, the emergence of a third kind of space, a *transitional* space.

Transitional space

The inherent compulsion towards reducing the time-space frame of the process of industrialisation creates at a certain moment a third phase in the hierarchical relationship of the three subsystems of architecture. The turning point from a sequential space to a parallel space was still ambiguous; the shift from a parallel space to a subsequent type of space on the other hand is clearly noticeable. I would like to call this space a 'transitional' space. Construction is now actually creating the context, and both context and construction become one subsystem (see Figure 5.4).

Marc Auge has noted that in these transitional spaces there is no more duality, no more regret for something lost, as the modern artist lamented. He writes: 'Place and non-place [*his term for the transitional space*] are rather like opposed polarities: the first never completely erased, the second never totally completed' (Auge 1995: 79). Michel Foucault must have had something similar in mind when he wrote about a heteropia: 'capable of juxtaposing in a single real place several spaces, several sites that are in themselves incompatible ... they have a function in relation to all the space that remains' (Foucault 1986: 22).

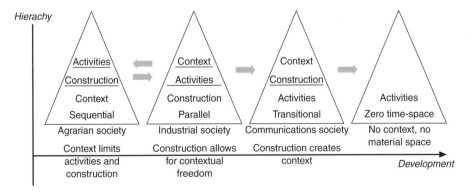

Figure 5.4 The shift towards transitional space

Once a transitional space has been introduced, the difference is clear between it and all other space. The scattered spaces that remain are by their very nature extremely introvert, allow often only restricted access and operate on a global 24-hour clock. A transitional space is in Umberto Eco's words a 'Fortress of Solitude' (Eco 1986: 3)—a place of transit with a strange illusion of rest and timelessness. We only have to think of casinos, airports, 24-hour shops, hotel chains, and airport lounges that are basically no-context spaces. The relationship of space to the context is completely different from the relationship of sequential or parallel space to its surroundings. The transitional space of a city like Las Vegas is, as Eco observed: 'not a city like the others, which communicate in order to function, but rather a city that functions in order to communicate' (Eco 1986: 40).

Transitional spaces are:

> . . . transit points and temporary abodes . . . proliferating under luxurious or inhuman conditions (hotel chains and squats, holiday clubs and refugee camps. . .); where a dense network of means of transportation, which are also inhabited spaces, is developing.
>
> (Auge 1995: 78)

Jean Baudrillard sees in these new spaces of extremes the dawn of a new world. Transitional spaces are 'the measure of our times' (Baudrillard 1986: 43) and the global business executive is spending more and more time in these transitional spaces, moving from one transit to the next, bridging thousands of kilometres. Rem Koolhaas sees the appearance of a new kind of creature for whom 'the muffled sound of planes . . . is a ubiquitous . . . element of the environment' (Wolf 2000: 310). The transitional space is the place that Koolhaas calls home, as he too spends 300 days a year in hotel rooms. Not only is the executive spending a great deal of his time in these transit zones, where everyone is on their way to somewhere else, many of us are spending or going to spend more and more time in these transitional spaces. In a city like Tokyo, for instance, the loss of space is being replaced by a confetti of transitional spaces. The enormous centralisation of business, institutions, universities and accommodation creates the well-known hyper-concentration of Tokyo. The lack of space, in turn, decentralises the various activities like working, eating, sleeping and relaxation to an extreme extent (van der Linden 2000a: 22). The influence of transitional spaces on corporate architecture is, as we will see later, phenomenal not only in Tokyo but anywhere.

The problems facing corporate architecture

Progress and modernisation

The idea of progress that we have described so far comes from the reduction of the time-space frame. For Richard Buckminster, fuller technological progress was the key to his own Taylorist technocratic thinking. Having gained bitter experience of the resistance to innovation while working as a travelling salesman selling new building materials, he noted a gestation lag between the invention and the use of new products. This lag differs from industry to industry; for electronics he noted a 2-year gap, for the airplane industry 5 years, in the automobile industry 10 years, railroading about 15 years, and for the skyscraper building industry it was 25 years (Pawley 1990: 25).

It is interesting to note that these gaps between invention and use depend on the industry, and even more interesting to see that they are reduced according to our general hypothesis that the process of modernisation is striving to decrease the time-space frame. Even more surprising is the fact that technological progress is following random, irrational paths. (Brian Arthur has also found some complex structures and patterns in economics; and I am currently studying the role that analogy plays in the progress of design and tracing its complex patterns (van der Linden 2000b).)

Benchmarking

Today the gestation lags are getting even shorter; in fact they are the key issue to success. Companies are benchmarking their operations in order to understand where they stand in relation to their competitors within their industry. Ironically, Taylor was arguably an early benchmarker in his studies to improve productivity. Today, companies often discover that they are losing ground as their competition can fabricate the same product in half the time, for half the cost. Benchmarking is an 'opportunity for organisations to gather, analyse and use information to raise their performance to the next level (Mah 2000: 1). Ernst & Young Real Estate Group published a report called 'Measuring Performance, Turning Silver into Gold.' In it they state:

> Change is inevitable. It surrounds us and its pace is increasing almost exponentially, fundamentally altering the way in which we carry out our business in the construction industry.
>
> (Bannon 1998: 1)

This pace of change is what Botond Bognar sees as creating the ephemeral nature of Japanese buildings. He gives examples of buildings that were pulled down without ever having been used (Bognar 1992: 9). The Japanese architect Toyo Ito openly acknowledges the fact that his structures are designed for merely a period of years, not decades (Bognar 1992: 9). This fate can be seen in office buildings as well. Tokyo has the world's largest office market of almost 76 million square metres. Tokyo also has almost twice as much vacant office space as Hong Kong has available office space (*Colliers Halifax Japan Update* 1999: 1). It seems that offices are therefore in line with computers and become outdated almost as soon as they are built.

Change

The reasons why these offices age so increasingly quickly are complex. The rapid changes taking place in technology, on the one hand, puts a lot of pressure on older buildings. More and more equipment is being introduced into the office, all of which is creating a burden on the infrastructure of these buildings. Offices often have air-conditioning systems that were not designed to take the extra amount of heat-load, the so-called heat islands created by excessive equipment. Another problem area is cabling. The cabling infrastructure that computers require, from the odd computer per 10 persons 15 years ago to one or more per person today, cannot be accommodated. Then the high land-prices and reports from benchmarking exercises often call for alternative occupancy plans with higher densities, again putting pressure on the mechanical and electrical systems. Older buildings, and we are sometimes talking about buildings constructed merely 10 years ago, often have, in addition to all these issues, a structural grid that is too narrow to allow for easy flexible planning.

Steward Brand (1994) observed in *How Buildings Learn* that the various layers of a building have a different cycle of physical change. Interestingly, these changes are all again in line with our theory of reducing the time-space frame by the process of industrialisation. The first layer, according to Brand, is the site, the geographical setting of a building that is the most timeless. Next there is the structure, the foundation and the load-bearing elements with a life span of 30 to 300 years. The skin, for offices mostly a glass curtain wall, changes every 20 years. Services, such as HVAC air conditioning, lifts, wiring, sprinklers and plumbing, wear out or become inadequate every 7 to 15 years. The need to change the interior plan often depends on the lease contract and ranges from 1 to 3 years. The furniture, phones and equipment can often change daily (Brand 1994).

First conclusion

In a similar diagrammatic way as we showed the transition from context to space in the shift from sequential space to parallel space (Figure 5.4), we can now see a change of emphasis in the four variables of the office. The new technology, changes in society, benchmarking results, and ideas from gurus like Peter Drucker and Franklin Becker, force companies to adopt new ideas that call for the flattening of the structure, and a new emphasis on strategic objectives, work process and culture, and individual and team awareness of company success. These issues—the re-engineering of the office—are now slowly translated into an office design. What is noticeable is that for many companies the emphasis of work still very closely relates to the variable space.

Alternatives to offices

As we saw before, the apparent need for the systemisation of work, the division of functions into a departmentalised environment, has led to an exaggerated linkage of function with space. I will repeat the old definition of the office: an orderly organised working environment, where each department, together with its files and clerks, are systematically accommodated.

Becker's 'Reinventing the Workplace' (Becker and Joroff 1995) examined the nature of this definition in order to implement new, alternative workplace strategies. Ernst & Young pioneered an alternative office method called 'hotelling' and eliminated the desks of 500 consulting employees. The savings in real estate cost on a project like this are tremendous, as for every five employees, only one desk is needed. Most of Ernst and Young's consultants are, for most of their working days, at the offices of their clients. In a hotelling scenario these consultants make a reservation for an office desk at the Ernst & Young office only to check their mail, attend internal meetings, etc., before they move on to the next job (Brill 1992: 24).

'Your office is where you are', by Philip Stone and Robert Luchetti (1985), anticipated these changes, predicting an upside-down, top-heavy organisational pyramid where the variable 'space' is becoming very variable indeed. Here, then, the office is becoming transitional, as it can be located anywhere— in the car, a restaurant, the client's office, in a hotel, an airport lounge, the aeroplane and so on. Indeed, studies show that individual workplaces today are never completely occupied (Frank 1994: 47). Over a period of a year, or 8,760 hours, most offices are only occupied for about 2,000 hours. This means a non-occupation level of 77 per cent!

Looking back at our scale of the four variables (Figure 5.2) we must remember that the costs related to the facility come second only to personnel cost. It seems obvious that our old notion of linking function directly to space is too excessive and too expensive:

> On average, real estate makes up 25 percent of the corporate assets of a Fortune 500 company; the cost of real estate can be as much as 15 percent of a company's gross sales. Especially today, the corporate function is too costly not to be optimised.
>
> ('Corporate Real Estate: Building a Strategic New World', *Management Review*, February 1995.)

Second conclusion

The cost of real estate might be high but the objective value of the facility has dropped dramatically. In terms of perception, at least, there has been a shift in the office from the variable of 'space' to the variables of 'technology' and 'people.'

The high degree of benchmarking has turned the office, and especially the facility management department, into something like a cost centre. As office space is now seen as an easy way to reduce costs (the facility department, after all, does not contribute to making profit), all that facility managers seem able to do is to reduce expenses. Furthermore, implementing alternative office strategies like hotelling or desk sharing seems like an easy way to reduce operating cost while implementing new management theories (Stungo 1996: 8). Theories that state that the office can be anywhere, ironically emphasise a kind of uselessness of the originally static office. Not only are the theoretical arguments made in support of this view very convincing, but so are the financial ones.

Technology, to a large degree, makes these changes possible and is moving at Internet-speed. Today's buildings, designed with function uniquely projected into space, are, however, too static to accommodate these rapid changes. So again we might ask ourselves whether we still need corporate architecture?

Office change

New workplace design

The new ideas that were developed in the early 1990s regarding management and organisational change addressed mainly strategic objectives, work process issues, work culture issues, and the increasing emphasis on the individual. Michael Brill has investigated the link between these new management ideas and the design of the new workplace intended to accommodate these changes. Between 1994 and 1999 Brill's consultancy firm, Bosti, carried out research that involved approximately 12,000 people in seventy organisations. The conclusions from this investigation included the following.

* Workplace design has a far greater effect on individual productivity, team productivity and job satisfaction than previously believed.
* The emphasis on the flexibility of furniture is too expensive and often not beneficial to the actual needs of an organisation.
* Teamwork is occasional and intense and poorly supported by the workplace.
* The individual's workplace is still a primary location, but work can happen anywhere and companies still miss the design implications of this point.

(Brill 2000a: 1)

Brill's conclusion, that workplace design has a greater effect on overall productivity than previously believed, addresses our problem statement directly: there is still a need for office space, but what is missing is linking of the design to changing needs. In order to understand this we need to examine the overall role of design.

Design

Design is part of the process of modernisation and, as we saw, it played an integral part in the shrinking of the time-space frame. Francis Duffy has noted the low entry level of design and he believes it should go 'beyond superficial styling'. Duffy defines office design as:

> ...the skilled and cost-effective allocation of physical resources to solve immediate as well as long-term accommodation problems—despite uncertainty, inadequate information and shifting goals—for users, clients and society at large in such a way as to embrace both high culture and deep practicality ... design corresponds to nothing more closely than the highest levels of strategic management.
>
> (Duffy and Tranis 1993: 9)

The fact that, according to Duffy, design should address the workplace as a strategic business tool is shared by many specialists in the field.

Carefully designing your office to support what people and teams actually do is, according to Brill, 'an investment that pays off in both business terms and in positive changes in corporate culture' (Brill 2000b). Pamela Brenner (1999) believes that the role of the workplace is the key to motivating and retaining knowledge workers, and Paul Siebert writes that 'teams are becoming today's essential work unit' (Siebert 1998: 2).

Design thus:

> ...becomes the art of recognising, defining and improving [the] relation-
> ships ... that change through the range of tasks and activities that define
> the work process. The approach to achieving this in a product is either
> through a user control feature or through self-adjusting properties that
> 'bend' with the user.

(Siebert 1998: 6)

However, designers, according to Siebert, find it difficult to actually formulate
a strategy for the adjustment of features.

This brings us back to one of the influential new management theorists,
Peter Drucker, who states that in order to know how to do a task you have to
ask the people who do it. This is what architects and designers need to understand: how the workplace can contribute to productivity, to recognise the
users' exact but changing needs and to translate this into the design of a
working environment that is supportive and flexible to the specific requirements of a corporation (Freiman 1994: 51).

The role of the architect

Now that the significance of design is clear, we need to address the practical
issues of design, and the role of the architect in conceiving the new work environments. In an article in 'Architecture' Barry LePatner, himself not an architect by profession, describes the diminishing role of the architect. In order to
resume the role of the 'Master Builder' (assumed by architects until the early
1970s), architects must redefine their practice and move:

> ...beyond merely serving as the client's project manager to becoming a
> direct participant in all elements of the client's building and human
> resource needs. The times demand that architects become full-time trusted
> advisors to their clients ... by asking the same kind of questions that exec-
> utives ask; and by studying their client's world with the same perspective
> of those decision makers.

(Le Patner 1998: 164)

In order to do this the architect must make more use of his multi-disciplinary
background that enables him/her to tackle the complex issues related to the
construction industry. Projects of any scale require a mix of technical, aesthetic, economic, structural, cultural, legal, and psychological knowledge. In
finding solutions to the problems faced by corporate architecture, described
above, the architect should apply a multi-disciplinary approach that bridges the

four variables and be able to show insight as to how each variable contributes to the overall goals and objectives of a company. The increasing trend towards transitionality will mean that the rigid mind-set of architects to provide solutions in construction drawings needs to be postponed or even deleted, as office design does not necessarily, any longer, mean building an office. Thus, in practical terms, the fact that fees are linked to the construction budget creates a conflict of interests when designing, for instance, alternative office strategies. New, more imaginative fee structures need to be employed, involving such arrangements as bonuses based on schedule, budget control, and stock options etc. Architects should see the fantastic opportunities that the new working environments offer.

Is this the kind of professional the consultancy firm Arthur Andersen is looking for when it posted this ad for a workplace transformation manager?

> Arthur Andersen ... view[s] the workplace as a strategic asset to support an enterprise's business objectives. The Workplace Transformation approach examines alternative business strategies, corporate cultures, management and human resource policies and technologies that affect the human environment. If you favour traditional methodologies in architecture, facilities management, environmental design, and business consulting, then go back to your cubicle. But if you favour a progressive approach to implementing landmark corporate solutions for the Fortune 50 companies making the headlines, then invent a better place to spend your day.
>
> (IDRC 2000)

The new field of operations

Keeping in mind the evolution that the design of the office has gone through, we need to consider certain design criteria. We can no longer refer to the traditional template when designing an office. Flexible, adaptive scenarios of spaces that keep an array of options open are what clients now expect from design. Based on our description of design, the architect will need, in order to fulfil these expectations, to monitor constantly the new and changing needs of his/her clients. Consequently, his/her advice should help employees perform better in these new, fluid, fast moving transitional spaces. The required office spaces will need to fulfil at least the following practical criteria:

- The floor load needs to be calculated to determine whether or not a floor can bear today's higher densities and office equipment.
- The floor-to-floor height needs to be enough to accommodate air-conditioning and raised floors for under-floor cabling. Alternatively, when renovating buildings with low ceilings, thin cooling ceilings can be installed.

- The building grid determines the flexibility and usability of the space and needs to be as wide as possible.
- Lifts have been the key to economic success since the Equitable building of 1870. Lifts need to be fast and calculated to accommodate the capacity of the building.
- More and more equipment requires more electrical power per square metre. The building should be able to accommodate these additional electrical power boxes.
- Cabling to support the network will require a substantial amount of vertical shaft and under-floor space.
- Studies have shown that lighting quality is becoming increasingly important, especially for computer work, as glare will cause wrong postures causing backaches and other muscular problems which have a direct influence on productivity. Furthermore, using energy efficient lighting can save running costs considerably.
- The criteria for the location of buildings are also changing; proximity to clients, vendors, distributors, transportation, and skilled labour are becoming prime considerations when corporations choose their office building.

Apart from these practical issues, we need to consider the fact that the process of modernisation will continue to bring space and time together. The rigid and slow process of design needs to change to be able to address the fuzzy matters of design.

- Similar to the conflict that occurred between sequential spaces and parallel spaces, the introduction of the new management ideas in the office environment will create friction between new thinking and the old styles of working that will continue to exist. This will cause a feeling of identity loss, comparable to the duality of feelings that the modern artist noticed in the early modern cities. Change and transition management will take an increasingly important role in the design of the working environment.
- The shrinking of the time-space frame will continue dramatically and this will generate uncertainty, as work will need to be performed at Internet speed. Technology will be the main force for pushing these changes.
- Transitionality will mean that more and more people will leave the office for short or longer business trips, working while they are on the move. Despite telecommunication technologies, face-to-face contact will remain a dominating business factor.
- New strategies will be needed to use and occupy space. Transitionality suggests that the office will become, to a greater extent, fragmented and all those fragments need designing. Airline companies, for example, noticed that their business lounges are being used as offices by executives, and have started to include fax machines, modems, and other business support

equipment and services to attract these transitional business people. Hotels have followed, coffee shops and fast food restaurants are becoming ever-popular in-between-meeting places to take notes, write memos and check emails.

• Flexible concepts regarding the use of space will need to be developed. Architects will have to design hotels like offices and offices like hotels.

Conclusions

The whole idea of a transitional society might have originated from Japan. A Japanese study group, established to provide economic planners with guidance as to where society is heading, introduced in the 1960s the term: *johoka shokai* or 'information society' (Meyers 1987: 677). According to the study, the level of (let us call it) 'the informationalisation of a society', is measured by the number and the rate of words produced and consumed. Analogous to this measure, a society's transitionality indicator will be the number of people working in the transitional spaces and the amount of time they spend in them. Information, technology and transitional spaces will become ever more entangled, as the same technology that is building and maintaining the information society is used to operate and give access to the transitional spaces, all of which will give new opportunities to business. These opportunities, however, require a deep understanding of the factors that drive the informational society and operate the transitional spaces.

References

Auge, M. (1995) *Non-places*, Verso: London.

Avrin, L. (1991) *Scribes, Script and Books*, London: The British Library.

Bannon, E. (1998) *Measuring Performance—turning silver into gold*, London: Ernst and Young Real Estate Group, http://www.eyuk.com, accessed 27/4/00.

Baudrillard, J. (1986), *Sideraal Amerika*, Amsterdam: 1001.

Becker, F. and Joroff, M. (1995) *Reinventing the Workplace*, Norcross, GA: International Development Research Council.

Berman, M. (1988) *All That is Solid Melts into Air*, New York: Penguin.

Bognar, B. (ed.) (1992) 'Between reality and fiction', *Japanese Architecture II*, *Architectural Design*, 99.

Bologna, G. (1988) *Illuminated Manuscripts*, London: Thames and Hudson.

Brand, S. (1994) *How Buildings Learn*, New York: Penguin Books.

Brenner, P.M. (1999), 'Motivating knowledge workers: the role of the workplace in quality', *Progress*, January.

Brill, M. (1992) 'Checking-in: the office as hotel', *Design Management Journal*, Spring.

—— (1994) *Now offices, no offices, new offices . . . wild times in the world of the office work*, Toronto: Teknion.

—— (2000a) 'Shifting perceptions in workplace design', *Alt.office Journal*, April 26, http://www.altoffice.com, accessed 13/11/00.

—— (2000b) Bosti Associates, homepage: economic benefits http://www.bosti.com/benefits.htm, accessed 9/8/00.

Colliers Halifax Japan Update (1999) http://www.colliershalifax.com/frame1.htm, accessed 27/4/00.

Cortoda, J.W. (1993) *Before the Computer*, Princeton, NJ: Princeton University Press.

Cowan, H.J. (1978) *Science and Building*, New York: John Wiley and Sons.

Delegado, A. (1979) *The Enormous File*, London: John Murray.

Duffy, F. and Tranis, J. (1993), 'A vision of the new workplace', *Site selection and industrial development*, April, reprinted in *Steelcase Workplace Knowledge*, http://www.steelcase.com/knowledgebase/avision.htm (accessed 27/4/00).

Eco, U. (1986) *Travels in Hyper-reality*, London: Picador.

Economist (1995) 'The white-collar factories', November 25.

Flood, R.L. and Carson, E.R. (1988) *Dealing with Complexity*, London: Plenum Press.

Foucault, M. (1986) 'Of other spaces', *Diacritics*, 16.

Frampton, K. (1987) *Modern Architecture*, London: Thames and Hudson.

Frank, S.B. (1994) 'Reinventing the architecture of work', *ID*, November: 27.

Freiman, Z. (1994) 'Hype vs reality: the changing workplace', *P/A*, March: 4.

Gordon, G. (1978) *System Simulation*, Englewood Cliffs, NJ: Prentice-Hall.

IDRC (2000) Job opportunity posting (Workplace Transformation Manager, Arthur Anderson, Inc, NY) http://site.conway.com/jobopps/jobdetail.cfm?ID=135, accessed 12/10/00.

Koolhaas, R. (1994) *Delirious New York*, Rotterdam: 010 Publishers.

LePatner, B.B. (1998) 'From velnerable to valuable', *Architecture*, March.

Linden, van der, M.A.L.C. (2000a) 'Tokio Transitioneel', *Telewerken*, January: 22.

—— (2000b) 'De Traditionel Stad', *Telewerken*, 1.

Mah, M. (2000) 'The multiple dimensions of metrics: metrics and the learning organization', *IT Metrics*, VI, 2, February: 1.

Meyers, R.A. (ed.) (1987) *Physical Science and Technology*, Orlando, FL: Academic Press.

O'Dea, W.T. (1958) *The Social History of Lighting*, London: Routledge and Kegan Paul.

Pawley, M. (1990) *Buckminster Fuller*, London: Trefoil Publications.

Siebert, P. (1998) 'New human factors', *American Centre for Design Journal*, 7: 1.

Stone, P.J. and Luchetti, R. (1985) 'Your office is where you are', *Harvard Business Review*, 63, 2: 103.

Stungo, N. (1996) *Inward Investment*, London: RIBA Interiors.

Travers, B. (1994) *The World of Invention*, Detroit, MI: Gale Research.

Weisman, W. (1970) in E. Kaufmann Jr. (ed.) *The Rise of an American Architecture*, New York: Praeger Publishers.

Wittfogel, K. (1957) *Oriental Despotism*, New Haven: Yale University Press.

Wolf, G. (2000) 'The unmaterial world', *Wired*, June: 310.

Part 3

The design and introduction of new methods of work

In Part 3 we examine two sets of frameworks for understanding and managing the introduction of new methods of work. Diana Limburg, in Chapter 6, reminds us that in addition to 'technically' oriented matters, the implementation of new work constructs, whether information systems or new forms of working, involve deep and often difficult organisational changes. Her argument is supported by the case of Compu-NL's introduction of telework. As with new innovations in general, telework can also be seen as a catalyst for greater change and organisational transformation and learning. As new organisational and working forms are introduced, learning must happen at the 'second order' level, as single-loop learning (relating to immediate work goals and practices) will not challenge the current organisational structures.

Communication is a key factor in securing success, Limburg argues. Introducing telework needs constant and intensive organisational argumentation, in which good initiatives are being advanced and bad ones eliminated. For Limburg, design is a 'pivot' in the learning process, with new organisational forms needing to develop over time. Perhaps the most important message of the chapter is that telework introduction is a complicated and demanding task that should be carefully managed. Good management in this case is a combination of guidance and openness for new solutions, with design aspects serving as a catalyst of organisational change more generally.

Chapter 7 by Wendy Spinks continues the focus on work design but concentrates on issues in the Japanese context. The basic building blocks of Japanese working conditions are set out by Spinks in her account of the 'three trinities'. The first trinity consists of long-term employment, a system based on seniority and strong company unions. This is more or less known already by most Western readers. Less known might be the notions of ambiguous job descriptions, on-the-job training and fuzzy job evaluation that form the second trinity. Together these mean that evaluation based on performance is often not appropriate in Japanese workplaces, a matter that may provide a poor basis for the introduction of new ways of working, such as telework. Another hindrance to telework is the strong group orientation of Japanese society; this means that each teleworker has to maintain strong group relationships, which is not easy over distance.

In her chapter, Spinks identifies the emergence of an embryonic third trinity. This, she says, encompasses contract-based employment, evaluation systems based on performance and merit, greater autonomy for workers and more organised workplace support along side on-the-job training. However, as the current workplace structures are deeply rooted in the Japanese society, fast changes cannot be expected.

Spinks' conclusions are similar to those of Limburg in that telework implementation cannot take place overnight because it is a complicated and demanding task. Structural legacies need to be taken into account, with internal human resource management departments needing to adopt the role of change agents.

6 Realising new organisational forms

Integrating design and development in the change process

Diana Limburg

Introduction

Developments in the competitive environment of organisations as well as in technology (in particular ICT) urge organisations to reconsider their form, for example, by introducing eBusiness or by becoming a virtual organisation. ICT serves as an enabler for these new work developments, with demands from the environment providing the motivating force (e.g. Igbaria and Guimaraes 1999). A key term for the new work developments is 'flexibility', first, because management has a wider choice of forms to achieve a fit with the environment and, second, because the new organisational forms allow for more *operational* flexibility.

The focus of this chapter is on how existing organisation that is no longer adequate can be changed into the desired new, flexible organisation. This is not a matter simply of implementing a technology. Achieving actual change means that a new way of working is incorporated in the daily routines of the organisation. Changing organisations is notoriously difficult—even more so when fundamental changes in work routines are necessary, as with introducing eBusiness and virtual organisations. In this chapter we will use one of the new flexible work forms, namely teleworking, as an example. Because the impact of telework on the organisation is, on aggregate, similar to the impact of other new forms of work, we will extrapolate the experiences of teleworking to all new organisational forms.

In the first section we will argue why telework will have a substantial impact on the organisation. Based on these arguments we will then discuss which approach to the introduction process is most appropriate. The method that is thus developed will be applied to the case of the introduction of telework at Compu-NL. In the final section we will draw some lessons from the case study for the introduction of new flexible organisational forms in general.

The impact of introducing telework

Introducing telework to an organisation implies a change in the temporal-spatial structure of an organisation (van der Wielen *et al.* 1993; Kompast and Wagner 1998). Employees are allowed, forced, or encouraged to work (part-time) at a location other than the traditional office, usually supported by modern information and communication technology (ICT). The existing temporal-spatial structure of an organisation has evolved over time, and is important for the work routines and social contacts within an organisation (Giddens 1985). For example, offices provide desks with computers to do the routine work, but they also form a context for social interaction, as colleagues come to the same office to do related work. For the purpose of interaction, colleagues from the same department are usually located near each other. If not, interaction is often scarce, even within the same office. To see telework as just transporting information instead of people is, therefore, at the very least incomplete, as it only refers to the office as a place for (routine) activities, and not as a place for *social* interaction.

Becker and Steele (1995) quote the anthropologist Hall (1959) who links the status impact of an office to the 'silent language': a wide range of messages, such as the identity of users and of the group as a whole; the history of the organisation (key people, critical events), and leaders' values about relationships, work processes, important goals and the like; expectations about what should and should not happen in the place; and messages about who should and should not use it. Changing the use of the office space, or the place where work is done, will inherently remove or change references to the old identity, history and values. This implies that things that were obvious before have to be reinvented or redeveloped. There is a close relation between organisational culture, values and beliefs, and the place and time where work is carried out. Therefore, having employees working (part-time) remotely from each other not only defines the place where they are working (location), but can also be a statement of trust, of flexibility, and so forth. This indicates that implementing telework can have a major impact on the organisation and its employees. Old routines will become obsolete; new routines will have to be developed.

Because telework influences these intangible, silent aspects of the organisation, a telework situation cannot be completely designed. After all, designing requires explicit description of the envisioned future situation, which is not possible for these intangible aspects. So, many aspects of the new organisational form will have to develop over time. At this level of aggregation, other types of new organisational forms are comparable to telework. Many of the new organisational forms also imply changes in the temporal-spatial structure of the old situation, as is the case when introducing virtual work teams. Some aspects of the new form can be designed, for example, procedures on how team-members will be selected, and what technology will be supplied to support communication. Other aspects, such as mechanisms for building and expressing trust, will have to develop over time.

The change process

From the previous section it has become clear that a method that will guide the process of introducing telework in an organisation will have to take into account the fact that aspects of the new organisational form will have to develop over time, and cannot be designed. On the other hand, a method that only aims at development will not be specific enough, as such methods are not intended to reach a particular organisational form (e.g. Organisational Development as described by French and Bell 1990). In this section we will examine which existing methods combine design and development and are suitable for supporting the introduction of telework.

Situated design

As a first step in finding a method for introducing telework, we chose the 'situated design' approach (Greenbaum and Kyng 1991). Greenbaum and Kyng summarise their approach in the following points (Greenbaum and Kyng 1991: 15):

- The design process needs to start with an understanding of the use situation (designers and users learn about each other's basic assumptions).
- When computer systems are introduced within an organisation, they change the organisation; likewise computer systems[1] adapt as they are used. Systems should, therefore, be designed for ongoing change.
- The design process is firmly rooted in experience, not just in rules.
- Users are competent practitioners.

This approach not only combines design and development, but also explicitly pays attention to user participation. Greenbaum and Kyng (1995) recommend the use of reflective action, or a co-operative approach to bridge the gap between design and development. The 'users' (any organisational members who come into contact with the change) will comment not just upon paper designs and proposals, but a design (prototype) will actually be introduced into their daily work. The real life of the organisation will reveal problems and opportunities in the design, and employees and designers will together reflect on these. Based on this reflection, the initial design can be adapted, and also the users can carry through changes in their way of doing work. This approach resembles an evolutionary use of prototyping (Hardgrave *et al.* 1999). Figure 6.1 illustrates the basic idea of this process.

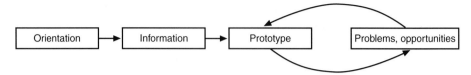

Figure 6.1 Evolutionary design

First of all, somewhere in the organisation the idea occurs that telework could be interesting. Before making this public an orientation takes place: could telework contribute to one or more organisational goals? Then information is gathered in the organisation, to find out what the current situation is, and what changes need to be made. Based on this information, a prototype is introduced and used. During use, problems and opportunities occur, which can then lead to actions to change the prototype. Thus, slowly, the prototype evolves into a full-grown new situation.

Learning as communication tool

When we studied and analysed the case of EduInfo (described in Limburg 1997) we found that the use of an evolutionary prototype, together with the ideas of situated design, is, in practice, too vague to support the process of introducing telework. Most importantly, it was impossible to achieve a fluent transition from the pilot study (which we regarded to be the prototype) to a full implementation throughout the entire organisation. The pilot has to finish at some moment, to be followed by further implementation, if successful. Furthermore, it is felt that at some point the telework design should be more or less final, otherwise administrative tasks will become complicated, and other daily processes will remain unstable—a situation that is undesirable for both external and internal customers. On the other hand, even after 2 years of teleworking, people still make changes to their work routines, since, for example, their environment has finally become used to teleworking. There should therefore still be room for changes in the final design, for specific individual cases and other developments in and around the organisation.

We accumulated these insights into a more refined and specific method for the introduction of telework, as illustrated in Figure 6.2. The process described in this model starts with orientation and information stages (that are not depicted), in the same way as the first, crude model. Based on the information gathered during these stages, a pilot design is created, preferably as a joint effort by all parties involved, and based on general understanding (literature) and organisation-specific knowledge (surveys, interviews, discussions, internal experts) regarding telework. This pilot design will be introduced into part of the organisation. During the daily routines, individuals will learn a new way of working while, at the same time, experiencing aspects of the design that could be improved. Some improvements will be made immediately; others will have to wait to be incorporated into the final design. Not only has the individual to learn but the group will have to acquire new routines too. The yields of this phase will be higher if exchange of experiences takes place. Also, the experiences should be documented for the final design, and for informing the future users of the final design. After a certain period of time (usually 4 to 6 months) all experiences will be collected and put into use in the final design (as far as possible). Though the final design is 'final', every new teleworker will still have to learn this new way of working, and every new situation will bring about new experiences that might have to be incorporated into the design (this then becomes development). It is also important to note that many difficulties in daily routines (that may be acceptable in a pilot situation) will not be acceptable in a final design. Novice teleworkers will be able to learn from experienced teleworkers.

Learning and organisational change

In the previous section we have introduced learning as a communication tool, to explain what happens in the organisation when the design is adopted and adjusted to the work situation. In this section we will further elaborate on the meaning of learning for organisational change processes. Dodgson states that there is rarely agreement as to what learning is, both within and between disciplines (Dodgson 1993: 376). Learning relates to both process and outcomes, and it can be described as the ways firms build, supplement and organise knowledge and routines around their activities and within their cultures, and

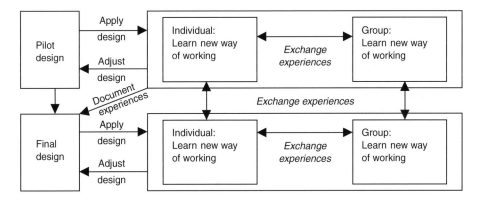

Figure 6.2 Learning during pilot and final design

adapt and develop organisational efficiency by improving the use of the broad skills of their workforce (Dodgson 1993: 377). In the context of this chapter we refer to the second part of this definition, where learning plays a role in improving the performance of an organisation. This can happen continuously (a learning organisation) and as a part of a change process, and learning can take place at different levels. Usually a distinction is made between single-loop learning and double-loop learning (or higher order learning) (Argyris and Schön 1978). Single-loop learning involves making improvements within the existing set of principles, assumptions and paradigms. Double-loop learning means that new principles, assumptions, and paradigms are adopted. The intro-duction of telework and other new organisational forms requires such higher order organisational learning, because the changes to the temporal-spatial structure require new routines to be developed. But it also involves first-order learning, when new principles are tailored to the situation and to daily changes.

Like situated design, learning can build a bridge between design and devel-opment. This idea is used by Robey *et al.* (1995), by incorporating business process redesign (BPR) into organisational learning (see Figure 6.3). From an organisational learning perspective, a design operates as an enabler (and dis-abler) of *learning*, and change takes place incrementally. This contrasts with the starting point of BPR, which is that change is radical. This approach:

> ...conceives of business process reengineering as a component of the more general process of organisational learning. Organisational learning provides the rationale for change as well as insights into how such changes may be implemented; reengineering focuses on the tools for converting planned objectives into realised form.
>
> (Robey *et al.* 1995: 35)

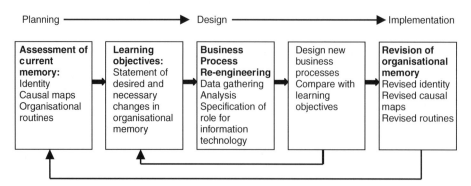

Figure 6.3 Business process re-engineering as a component of the organisational learning process, in Robey *et al.* (1995: 36)

This learning process starts with the assessment of the current memory (identity, causal maps, organisational routines), and the establishment of objectives for change. These will provide a shared understanding of where the implementation process should lead. Based on the information from the first stage, a design is made, which will subsequently provoke changes. It will also occur in the middle of changes, some parts being rather fixed, others changing while the organisational members are learning, thus changing their interpretative schemes. The first stage is a form of self-reflection—in organisational learning terms, establishing identity, causal maps and organisational routines. The importance of this self-reflection is also stressed in the rules for situated design. Paying sufficient attention to agreeing on the (learning) goals of the change process and discussing the current situation helps to prevent a danger that, according to Cooprider and Henderson (in Stein and Vandenbosch 1996) exists in evolutionary prototyping, whereby:

> ...the system builder and user will come to agreement on a solution before they have fully evaluated all of the systems requirements.
>
> (Stein and Vandenbosch 1996: 117)

After the design phase, another type of learning takes place during the process of implementation. The newly designed processes must be accepted and shared as revisions to organisational memories. According to the ideas of situated design, in this phase the design itself can also change. This is also consistent with ideas behind structuration theory:

> ...human action can be seen on the one hand to constitute the institutional properties of social systems, yet on the other hand it can be seen to be constituted by institutional properties.
>
> (Orlikowski and Robey 1991: 147)

In other words, a design is created (routines, procedures, technology) which is released into the daily work, changing the social system. Exposed to these daily routines, the design is changed too, for example, because something that is at first new will gradually become routine. This is also one of the principles of situated design, as mentioned earlier: computer systems and organisation influence each other during use. Stein and Vandenbosch (1996) also refer to this link between learning and structuration theory. They state that organisational learning can be seen as a subset of interactions that may be said to contribute to structuration (Stein and Vandenbosch 1996: 118). For double-loop learning to take place, the design, and the change management, should provoke and support double-loop learning, which occurs when members question underlying assumptions and norms, and modify their shared maps and theories in use (interpretative schemes).

For the change process, it is important to realise that the design is a pivot in the learning process. It should therefore be made with maximum learning value. The communication during the process of making the design and implementing the design should also be aimed at learning from the (experiences with the) design. During the change process it should be stressed that the design is not the final answer to a problem, but a tool to support the learning process that will lead to an improved organisation.

Ang *et al.* (1997) studied three consecutive IT-implementation projects in one organisation to learn about the relation between IT-implementation and organisational learning. Based on their findings, they adapted the model proposed by Robey *et al.* because they found that technical knowledge on how IT will impact business processes is necessary for change. In the introduction of telework, this can be translated as the necessity of acquiring knowledge about the relationship between time-space structures and the organisation. Therefore, a model to support the introduction of telework should also incorporate this knowledge.

Review

The similarities between approaches to organisational learning, situated design and the ideas of structuration theory are striking. Together they lead to the following conclusions:

- Introducing telework requires higher-order learning, because users have to modify their shared maps and theories in use; first-order learning is also necessary for modifying the design to the situation.
- Three main steps should be taken to change a situation towards telework: self-reflection (consisting of identifying the current situation and the learning objectives), design, and revision of memory (learning).
- The design should be made such that it stimulates learning, by provoking users to question underlying assumptions and norms.
- Knowledge about telework is essential to the change process.
- The change process should be managed according to these principles and the learning process should be facilitated and guided.

Combined, these conclusions lead to a revised method for the introduction of telework, that is graphically represented in Figure 6.4. Central in this model are the stages based on the work of Robey *et al.* Underpinning these stages is the body of telework knowledge which should be consulted at each stage. Moreover, this body of knowledge is further augmented and refined at each step, since organisation-specific knowledge and experience are continually gathered. Alongside every stage is the necessary support for the process.

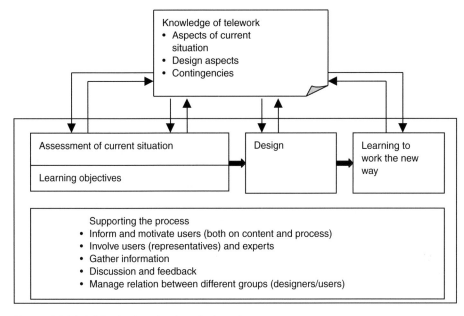

Figure 6.4 Model for the introduction of telework

Telework design

The telework design and, more generally, knowledge about teleworking, will play an important role in the change process, as we have concluded in the previous section, and a good design will stimulate learning. Also the design reflects part of the knowledge about telework that is so important for the change process. Therefore this section will be dedicated to telework design. The knowledge of telework will also be used for the first phase of the change process—self-reflection. This is because it helps to get a telework-directed view on the current situation and on the learning objectives. In this section we will provide a short overview of the impact of telework and the design options available, based on their impact on the temporal-spatial structure.

The impact of telework on the organisation

Knowledge of the impact of telework on the organisation is needed to guide the process of assessing the current situation and making a design. It will help management to know what aspects are important to study, and what problems and opportunities call for which design features. Here a short overview is given of the impact of telework on the organisation, based on the starting point that changes will be made in the time/space structure.

Performing individual tasks

Employees have a set of different tasks, each with different demands with regard to time and place modes. Introducing telework gives an opportunity to achieve a better fit between demands of tasks and the available modes, but also reduces presence availability and changes the role of the office. Aspects that have to be taken into consideration when introducing telework are communication, access to information, the workplace, task division, and social contacts.

Working together

Most employees depend on colleagues in order to succeed in their work, either because each performs one step in a process or because they need each other's expertise. Being in the same place at the same time (co-presence) facilitates co-operation. Here the most important aspects are communication, task division, and social contacts.

Managing groups/departments

Managing is both related to supporting individuals in doing their jobs and supporting/encouraging members of departments to work together. Managers have to view the department's work in the perspective of the whole organisation and vice versa. Many features of offices are aimed at easing the task of the manager (see Kompast and Wagner 1998). The most important factors related to management are communication, leadership style, and social contacts.

Contingency factors

Further elaboration upon these items, combined with gains that can be attained, lead to a list of contingency factors (see also Limburg 1998) that influence the feasibility of telework in a specific organisation. Studying the contingencies can help management to decide whether a situation is more or less favourable for (certain forms of) teleworking. An organisation can use a categorisation of telework situations (e.g. Qvortrup 1998) to get a first insight, as these categories can easily be associated with one's own type of work and organisation. The first step of management would be to get a broad idea of what type of telework would fit best. Next, all contingencies have to be studied separately. This analysis has two goals: first, to see how (un)favourable the situation is and, second, to identify contingency gaps that will have to be covered in the design. Hence, a close relationship exists between the contingencies and the telework design.

Design options

To achieve a 'teleworking design' that fits a given situation, several aspects of technology, organisation and work can be influenced. In other words: a design can be made, consisting of several building blocks, which together constitute the tangible side of a new organisational form that can be categorised as 'telework'. The specific situation indicates which building blocks are available, which building blocks are useful, and how the building blocks should be shaped. As in a jigsaw puzzle, the shape of one piece is dependent on that of other pieces. For example, whether an organisation can implement the rule that email has to be checked every hour, depends on the network conditions. We distinguish five types of design options: ICT, Location, Rules and regulations, Agreements, and job Redesign. In Figure 6.5 we list examples of design options in each of these categories.

In the next section, we describe and analyse the case of Compu-NL in order to study the value of this method for the introduction of telework (combining process and content) in practice.

ICT	Location	Agreements
• Access to organisation's network (to access anything that can also be used at office + additional tools) • Office phone at home • (Software) tools to support co-operation over a distance (CSCW, teleconferencing) • Portable equipment (laptop computer, mobile phone) • Intranet	• What locations are available for what activities • Planning • How are locations equipped • Archive	The range of possible agreements is too large to give a complete overview, I will use the set of aspects earlier described to give an indication. • Performing individual tasks • Workplace • Task division (temporary) • Working together • Managing • Social contacts • At home (e.g. access to the workroom, schedule)

Rules and Regulations	Redesign of jobs
• Who (conditions under which any individual is allowed to telework) • Who is entitled to what equipment/services • How often (how many days a week, usually only maximum, also possible minimum (to justify investment for example) • Who pays what • Insurance and liabilities • Working conditions • Contract accommodations • Norms for accessibility and service-level to clients • Norms for amount of office space, number of desks, administrative support, etc.	• Creation of new jobs ○ Administrative support in general ○ Telework co-ordinator • Creation of new tasks ○ Extra workload; e.g. secretary sends all mail to home-address and checks incoming mail for urgency; helpdesk also supports problems at home ○ Exchange for other tasks; the pool of secretaries is expanded with a typist, to lower the burden • Permanent shift of tasks Tasks that cannot be done remotely are concentrated in jobs at the office and vice versa

Figure 6.5 Design options for telework

Combining design and learning: a case study

Background

Compu-NL is the Dutch branch of a large international organisation in the field of information processing systems, products and services. Over 4,000 people are employed, with this number rising. The teleworking project at Compu-NL mainly concerns sales-staff (approximately 2,000 employees). Headquarters of sales are in Amsterdam; clients, as well as the employees, are based all over the Netherlands. Desk sharing was introduced for sales staff in 1992; employees had the possibility of working from home before, although this was not really incorporated into the work situation. In April 1997 renewed interest in telework occurred, due to an increasing pressure on property costs. Management thought telework should be introduced for all sales staff on a volunteer basis. Employees were very eager to be home-based, because of the stress and time wasting associated with daily travel and traffic jams. Partly basing their judgement on the experience of the previous attempt to introduce teleworking, the project sponsor and project team thought the introduction of large-scale telework should be seen as an important organisational change which would also require cultural change.

The first phase in introducing telework at Compu-NL took place within the sales department. A pilot study with 30 employees was conducted, from April till June 1998. The pilot was preceded by a survey, charting the current situation and expectations. During the pilot, short questionnaires were conducted via email, with a further, concluding survey conducted 4 months later. We have described this phase in an earlier paper (Limburg 1998). The pilot study showed that employees benefited greatly from telework, but that problems could occur with teamwork and management. At this stage the property department took over the project, and integrated it into a large-scale redesign of the workplace, aiming for better, more flexible and more efficient work support. We will describe and analyse how the teleworking part of this project was structured. This description is mainly based on the second pilot study, involving 125 participants. Where relevant, the follow-up to the pilot will also be described. At the end of June 2000 a total of 500 employees were teleworking; over 1,000 other employees had limited facilities for working from home.

Self-reflection

The self-reflection stage in the change process consists of two parts: the identification of objectives and the assessment of the current situation.

Identification of objectives

It is important to realise that this project was driven by two imperatives. First, the international management of Compu-International ordered flexible work-places to be introduced, and provided guidelines for this. This fitted with a general tendency in the organisation towards more mental and physical mobility. Second, the first pilot was inspired by the employees, who were very eager to work from home for two main reasons: less travelling and better working conditions. Thus, two types of objectives were already established. The pilot was not seen as a basis for a go-no go decision, but was rather aimed at gathering more knowledge on how telework would work in practice at Compu-NL and at enabling further improvement in the design; it was seen as a user support process in itself. Goals of the pilot, and of introducing telework, were discussed by the project team, which saw it as its responsibility to identify all aspects necessary for the successful introduction of telework on a large scale. But they also stressed the individual responsibilities of employees, management and several organisational functions to take appropriate measures.

A baseline survey (December 1998) was conducted to get an impression of the individual objectives of participants; this was done by asking open questions. As a supplement, participants were asked to explain why they participated in the pilot. The reason most given to both questions was of less travelling, followed at some distance by that of increased productivity and being able to concentrate better at home. The employees were also asked about expected drawbacks. The most important problem employees expected was of fewer social contacts or fewer opportunities of gaining informal information. They also expected problems with planning meetings and making appointments, separating work from private life and concerns about facilities at home. For Compu-NL, the fear was of less commitment—from colleagues, the department and Compu-NL generally—as well as less control and social isolation.

The survey was undertaken when most of the design for the pilot was complete. This was so as to be able to present the design to the participants, so that they could get a better impression of what to expect. Since a great deal of information was already available from the earlier pilot, and from the representatives of the user departments, the project team felt they had sufficient information to proceed with the design. In the survey, participants were also asked about their expectations by indicating to what extent they expected a decrease or increase in several aspects of their work life (e.g. time spent privately, productivity, contacts with manager). Employees expected to improve their productivity and quality of working conditions, and make more efficient use of time (e.g. less travelling). Managers expected higher employee motivation, better quality of working conditions and better fit between work and workplace. This inventory was intended to elicit a more detailed and detached impression of expectations. Later, real results could be compared to expectations. This information could then be used to improve support to new groups of users, since the difference between past expectations and results would be known. It is not really about setting goals, but neither is it really a part of assessing the current situation (although current expectations could be seen as part of the current mindset).

Members of departments were urged to discuss their expectations and their conditions collectively. Conditions, especially, can be seen as part of learning objectives. For example: we want to introduce teleworking in our department, but we do not want to lose teamwork. This brings us to the second aspect of self-reflection: assessment of the current situation.

Assessment of the current situation

The assessment of the current situation has two objectives: to be able to compare the future situation with the current situation, and to identify explicitly what is considered important in the current situation. As was discussed at the beginning of this chapter, and also explained to the participants, introducing telework would alter the space-time structures in the organisation; these before, naturally, helped the employees and managers to do their jobs, but also created problems. The assessment was done only at a local level, not for Compu-NL as a whole.

At the information meetings the departments were urged to discuss what they considered to be important aspects of being a department (what binds us) and what is expected from the manager. From the earlier pilot it had become clear that in many departments the managers' idea of her/his role was different to the employees' expectations, especially concerning the preservation of teamwork. Some departments reported that these discussions were very illuminating. Other departments never had them. The project team only saw it as their responsibility to bring the option of such discussions to the attention of the departments, not to enforce them. Another tool in assessing the current situation was the baseline survey. Questions were asked about individuals' personal situations, time spent working at home, working at clients' site and working at the Compu-NL office, time spent travelling, what activities were performed at which location, work situation (stress, motivation, importance of teamwork and informal communication), and means of communication. The results of these questions were used both by the departments themselves and by the project team to identify possible problems. Finally, one of the managers representing the users produced a document outlining the most important social aspects of introducing telework into his own department. This document was found to be very helpful and, therefore, was also distributed among the user representatives.

Reflection

The link between goal setting (what do you want from the future situation?) and expectations confirms our feeling that goal setting and assessment of the current situation are closely connected. People assess what is wrong with the current situation and, based on that assessment, they form ideas about a better future. If employees had been satisfied with the old situation, the idea of introducing telework would never have arisen. One stage of learning, therefore, had more or less taken place at the beginning of the process: identifying the need to change the theories in use. This made the learning objective rather straightforward: achieve a teleworking situation, in which departments can still function as a team. If the employees had been satisfied with the old situation, and it was only the higher management that wished to change, it would have been very difficult to communicate the learning objectives.

It appeared that effort put into goal setting and assessing the current situation was highly dependent on the effort of the individual managers. In general, there was less time available than the project team wished. Departments that put more effort into this process learned a great deal from it, although the other departments did not have many more problems. This might have been a lucky circumstance: the departments that did their best did not come up with very big problems anyway. Therefore handling the problems when they came along, as the other departments did, worked more or less satisfactorily. Sometimes the more enthusiastic departments were even less satisfied, for example when they identified problems and/or brought forward ideas and the project team did not react as they had expected. This might lead to the conclusion that if a general scan does not give the impression that big problems are to be expected, a more reactive, rather than proactive, approach should be recommended. This fits to some extent with situated design: let real life come up with situations that call for a reaction, then react if the situation is urgent enough.

Finally, some remarks should be made on the position of the pilot and the users in the pilot group. On the one hand, the pilot was part of the process of identifying objectives and assessing the current situation for Compu-NL as a whole. On the other hand, for the users in the pilot group, it involved the actual implementation of telework; therefore they went all the way in the learning process. However, they might be confronted with another design if, after the pilot, real changes had to be made to the design. This would mean that they would have to go through another stage of learning.

The design

A telework design consists of ICT, location, job design, rules and regulations, and agreements. In the case of Compu-NL, much work on the design had been done in the first pilot: for example, what equipment do people need at home (both ICT and furniture), how best to distribute equipment, what tax-arrangements are necessary and how should software be adapted? A great deal of feedback on the design aspects was therefore available from the operating situation. Most of the effort of the project team concerned the design, including (administrative) procedures, such as how to handle a call to the helpdesk from someone working from home. Optimising the design took more time than expected, delaying the start of people actually teleworking (officially and fully equipped). As in earlier cases, it became clear that accumulations of small problems regarding different aspects of the design, combined with (contradictory) wishes from different functions and user departments, resulted in a time-consuming design process. Many of the rules and regulations were designed centrally, although departments were free to add their own. Agreements were to be made locally, with the project team providing departments with ideas on which aspects of telework needed agreements (for example, distribution of mail), but the departments were left to undertake this. Thus this aspect of the design took place on the borderline between the next stage—learning—and the design itself. Job design was not really relevant in the user departments, but did take place in supporting departments, in connection with the issues such as: 'who is responsible for changing the software on the laptops?'.

After implementation, the design may change in two ways. First, aspects can be added locally, for example agreements or job design. Second, based on experience, changes can be made to central aspects such as procedures (e.g. who co-ordinates the installation of equipment in the home) or hardware (e.g. which printer to use).

A striking deficiency in the design was the lack of concrete action to support managers. From all evidence so far it was clear that the role of management was crucial, and possibly problematic. Therefore, the Human Resources (HR) department was asked to participate in the project team. It took a long time before a representative of HR was actively involved, even after this pilot period. In the meantime knowledge on the position of managers was communicated, but not translated into the design. In the final rollout, after the pilot, HR had a more distinct role. They had conversations with managers of departments that were about to be transformed and, based on these conversations, they suggest actions in various areas, for example training. The representatives of the HR department thought that introducing the telework design, especially concerning location, helped to enforce some changes that many people had wanted for some time. For example, managers had to change their style now, because they could no longer rely on visual control. For a long time, employees and managers had simply chosen to ignore suggested changes. However, these could no longer be ignored, because the building had changed and people no longer had a fixed workplace; they had to learn to work differently. This is a good example of how a design can provoke learning.

Learning to telework: learning to work the new way

As is clear from the final remark in the first subsection, for the users in the pilot group the learning stage occurred during the pilot but, for the other users, it was much later, after a (final) design had been made and implemented. Also, as we discussed, there is no clear demarcation between the learning phase and the design. It is helpful to define the transition from design to learning with the actual implementation of the hardware and procedures. That moment was different for all users, and took place between March and May 1999. The official start of the pilot study was set for April 1999. As explained in the previous subsection, this was much later than planned, which explains the long period between the baseline survey and the implementation of the design. This period of relative silence for the user created a discontinuity in the learning process that had started with the information meeting and the survey. Because those meetings were also much later than at first communicated with the participating departments, the delays caused irritation. One department even threatened to cancel its participation. They had first become convinced that introducing telework was important and urgent, now it seemed that their expectations were not considered important. It took much deliberation to keep this department on board.

During the pilot period, a trainee had several conversations with representatives of user groups, during which they articulated problems that occurred in practice. Many of these problems were not directly related to telework, though they appeared to be more urgent because of teleworking. The trainee discussed the results of the conversations with members of the project team. Some problems were followed up; others were left as they were. This created another episode of irritation—the representatives of the user departments had used some of their precious time to make an inventory of problems. They felt that their efforts were not fully appreciated by the project team. An important lesson from this is that the project team should not only be concerned with gathering information from the user situation for the final design, but should also be prompt in giving feedback on what they intend to do with the information from users' experiences. Though the approach chosen did to some extent bridge the gap between users and designers, each group (and subgroup) had its own agenda. Someone in the project team should have the task of ensuring that both groups remain aware of each other's worlds. This task can be combined with that of supporting the users.

Departments were again urged to discuss their experiences of telework during their regular meetings, and some departments acted on this advice. The project team stressed that it was important to talk about feelings, suggestions, irritations and needs, to prevent escalations. For example, if everybody acts as if it is normal to phone somebody at home at 11 pm, but individuals do not want to be disturbed then, this should be discussed. Even our mentioning this example created a sense of recognition.

Conclusions

This case shows that the steps derived from Robey *et al.* play an important role in the change process. The first stage, assessment of the current situation, combined with identifying the learning objectives, took place over a long period of time, during several stages of the project, and at different levels. We think the combination of a strong need from the employees, and a strong incentive from the international organisation, formed a winning combination. It made the learning goals clear at different levels; the employees were eager to do their best, and the higher level management was also involved. Often either one of these parties can be neutral or even negative. When studying the learning objectives for a telework project, an organisation and its employees can also agree on other methods to achieve the same ends as intended by teleworking. The idea of telework in itself helps to question the old assumptions, and thus opens people's eyes to other possibilities offered by ICT (Jackson 1998).

The assessment of the current situation is especially important at the local level, the level where routines have to change. For the project team, information on the current situation is important for the design and for the communication process. Because of the (learning) changes at the local levels, more all-encompassing changes can gradually take place. Many of these changes will have been in the pipeline for a long time, but might never have found a foothold. A combination of the learning goals and the compelling nature of the design can help establish this foothold. This confirms the status of the design as a pivot in the learning process. Because a telework design automatically changes the temporal-spatial structure of an organisation, people are forced to react. But, if they do not agree on the learning objectives, this could lead to fierce resistance and require (innovative) measures to work around an unpopular design (Orlikowski and Gash 1994).

Though the empirical study only concerns a situation in which telework has been introduced, we think we can safely extend the main conclusions to the introduction of other types of new organisational forms. The central argument for choosing the approach was that much of the new organisational form cannot be designed, but has to develop over time. This can best be done using a learning approach, in which the design serves as an impetus for actual change to occur. The learning process should not be left to itself, but should be carefully guided, providing all parties involved the opportunity to communicate their specific interests. This case has confirmed the importance of a shared learning goal, even if the motivations of different parties are different. It also shows that a good design can, indeed, trigger change. In conclusion we would recommend that managers use a combined learning-design approach to introduce a new form of organisation. The steps provided by Robey *et al.* are useful for this purpose. This general framework should, in each situation, be filled out with knowledge on the specific (type of) new organisational form. Accumulating this knowledge will help to improve further the success rate of implementations of new organisational forms.

Note

1 Greenbaum and Kyng refer to computer systems in their work, meaning mostly the technical side. We think their ideas are also applicable to sociotechnical systems like telework, amongst others, because they stress the links between IT and organisation themselves.

References

Ang, K.-T., Thong, J.Y.L. and Yap, C.-S. (1997) 'IT implementation through the lens of organisational learning: a case study of Insuror', *Proceedings of the Eighteenth International Conference on Information Systems*: 331–48.

Argyris, C. and Schön, D. (1978) *Organisational Learning: a theory of action perspective*, Reading, MA: Addison-Wesley.

Becker, F. and Steele, F. (1995) *Workplace by Design: mapping the high-performance workscape*, San Francisco: Jossey-Bass Publishers.

Dodgson, M. (1993) 'Organisational learning: a review of some literatures', *Organisation Studies*, 14, 3: 375–94.

French, W.L. and Bell, C.H. Jr. (1990) *Organisation Development: Behavioral Science Interventions for Organisation Improvement*, Englewood Cliffs, NJ: Prentice Hall International.

Giddens, A. (1985) 'Time, space and regionalisation', in D. Gregory and J. Urry (eds) *Social Relations and Spatial Structures*, New York: St. Martin's Press, 21–48.

Greenbaum, J. and Kyng, M. (1991) 'Introduction: situated design', in J. Greenbaum and M. Kyng (eds) *Design at Work: Co-operative Design of Computer Systems*, Hillsdale, NJ: Lawrence Earlbaum Associates: 1–24.

Hall, E.T. (1959) *The Silent Language*, New York: Fawcett World Library.

Hardgrave, B.C., Wilson, R.L. and Eastman, K. (1999) 'Toward a contingency model for selecting an information system prototyping strategy', *Journal of Management Information Systems*, 16, 2: 113–36.

Igbaria, M. and Guimaraes, T. (1999) 'Exploring differences in employee turnover intentions and its determinants among telecommuters and non-telecommuters', *Journal of Management Information Systems*, 16, 1: 147–64.

Jackson, P.J. (1998) 'Integrating the teleworking perspective into organisational analysis and learning', in P.J. Jackson and J.M. van der Wielen (eds) *Teleworking: International perspectives; from telecommuting to the virtual organisation*, London: Routledge, 245–57.

Kompast, M. and Wagner, I. (1998) 'Telework, managing spatial, temporal and cultural boundaries', in P.J. Jackson, and J.M. van der Wielen (eds) *Teleworking: International perspectives; from telecommuting to the virtual organisation*, London: Routledge, 95–117.

Limburg, D.O. (1997) 'The participatory design of telework at EduInfo', in P.J. Jackson and J.M. van der Wielen (eds) *Second International Workshop on Telework; Proceedings of the Workshop: 'Building Actions on Ideas, Amsterdam'*, Tilburg: Work and Organisation Research Centre, Tilburg University: 64–78

Limburg, D.O. (1998) 'Teleworking in a managerial context', in R.P. Suomi, P. J. Jackson, L. Hollmén and M. Aspnäs (eds) *Teleworking Environments, Proceedings of the Third International Workshop on Telework*, September 1–4, Turku, Finland: 93–106.

Orlikowski, W. and Robey, D. (1991) 'Information technology and structuring of organisations', *Information Systems Research*, 2, 2: 143–69.

Orlikowski, W. and Gash, C. (1994) 'Technological frames: making sense of information technology in organisations', *ACM Transactions on Information Systems*, 12, 2, 174–207.

Qvortrup, L. (1998) 'From teleworking to networking: definitions and trends', in P.J. Jackson, and J.M. van der Wielen (eds) *Teleworking: International perspectives; from telecommuting to the virtual organisation*, London: Routledge, 21–39.

Robey, D., Wishart, N.A. and Rodrigues-Dias, A.G. (1995) 'Merging the metaphors for organisational improvement: business process reengineering as a component of organisational learning', *Accounting, Management and Information Technology*, 5, 1: 23–39.

Stein, E.W. and Vandenbosch, B. (1996) 'Organisational learning during advanced system development: opportunities and obstacles', *Journal of Management Information Systems*, 13, 2: 115–36.

van der Wielen, J.M., Taillieu, T.C.B., Poolman, J.A. and Van Suilchem, J. (1993) 'Telework: dispersed organisational activity and new forms of spatial-temporal co-ordination and control', *European Work and Organisational Psychologist*, 3, 2: 145–62.

7 Structural legacies and flexible work

Japanese challenges

Wendy Spinks

Introduction

As electronically enabled forms of work become more commonplace and their potential fires the organisational imagination, it is sometimes easy to lose sight of the, perhaps, more pedestrian, yet crucial, issue of fit with the existing workplace. (While the term 'workplace' typically refers to the physical area in which work takes place and its layout, it is used in this chapter as a shorthand term for overall work and human resource management (HRM) practices in a given organisational setting. See Van der Linden's Chapter 5 for an in-depth discussion of the impact of physical workplace design on organisational context). Nevertheless, existing frameworks often have a critical impact on E-work adoption and, indeed, other forms of organisational change. If internal and external pressure towards structural inertia are as strong as Hannan and Freeman (1989), among others, claim, then a close examination of the existing workplace as the major source of internal constraints on structural change is more than warranted. This chapter is an attempt to examine certain aspects of such internal pressure, although it departs from the organisational ecology approach by focusing on a specific core of internal organisational character-istics, namely administrative systems and human resource management prac-tices (Donaldson 1995). In fact, this chapter's implicit undertone is perhaps better stated as a concern with the issue of organisational legacy or embedded-ness (Schein 1992), and its impact on structural fit and/or misfit. Specifically, it discusses at some length existing HRM practices in the Japanese corporate context and how HRM legacy affects the adoption of flexible work arrange-ments like telework. Before examining these issues, however, a brief overview of the current Japanese business climate is provided.

The changing organisational environment in corporate Japan

While the innovative nature of Japanese work practices on the manufacturing shop floor is relatively well-documented (for example, Total Quality Management, *kaizen* and just-in-time distribution), white-collar work practices in office-based settings have remained largely unchanged throughout Japan's high-growth period. The prolonged recession and increasingly swift penetration of information technology in the 1990s, however, are causing corporate Japan to rethink seriously its post-war patterns of white-collar employment and organisation. While the popular press has seen layoffs, bankruptcies and record levels of unemployment as presaging the 'collapse of the lifetime employment system', part of this corporate reassessment involves experimenting with flexible work arrangements in hitherto relatively rigid organisational structures. This chapter considers one example of workplace flexibility, namely telework, in an attempt to examine the impact of structural inertia on such change experiments. First, however, let us consider the broader background in which Japanese firms find themselves today.

The economy

Japan is no exception to the worldwide trend towards changing social contracts between employers and employees. The prolonged recession of the 1990s has triggered widespread reassessment of existing employment practices, graphically expressed in the form of extensive restructuring. The unemployment level not only hit an historical high of 4.9 per cent in 2000, but the relatively unknown phenomenon of newly minted university graduates being unable to find employment has given rise to new unemployment terminology. Whereas the traditional term for unemployment in Japanese is *shitsugyou* (literally 'loss of employment'), the term *mugyou* (literally 'no-work') is increasingly used to describe this unprecedented state of affairs. In a related move, the Japanese Ministry of Labour's *White Paper 2000* (Ministry of Labour 2000b) dedicated a special section to the growing phenomenon of 'freeters', young workers who spurn (either voluntarily or because they have no choice) traditional employment for positions of a more temporary nature (see Figure 7.1).

Elsewhere, business confidence is at an all-time low, with the number of corporate failures outstripping start-ups by an ever widening margin, rising fears over the integrity of the banking system, and the twin pressures of globalisation and the ICT revolution.

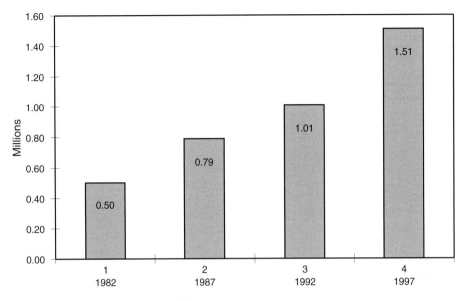

Figure 7.1 Estimated 'freeter' population

Source: Ministry of Labour's *White Paper 2000*: 151.

Demographic change

Demographic trends represent the single most important change factor in Japan. As has been widely documented, Japan is ageing faster than any other industrialised country. In fact, the percentage of Japanese of 65 years and over already hovers around the 15 per cent mark and is expected to reach 25 per cent early in this century. Such a rapid demographic shift will naturally have a significant impact on the social fabric as a whole.

In terms of the labour market, the most salient fact is that, despite today's unprecedented level of unemployment, in a few years Japan will be facing a labour shortage (government projections show the work force peaking in 2005). An even more sobering figure is that the number of Japanese under 20 years of age peaked in 1997 (see Figure 7.2). Such trends obviously mean that Japanese companies will have to turn to sectors they have traditionally shunned, namely women (of the OECD countries, Japan's female labour participation rate is considerably low—see Figure 7.3), elders, the disabled and foreign labour. Turning to such relatively untapped labour pools will undoubtedly strain established work patterns.

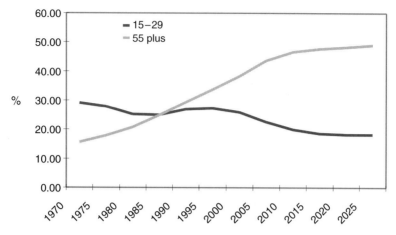

Figure 7.2 Labour force trends
(Adapted from Ministry of Labour *White Paper* 2000: 120, 133.)

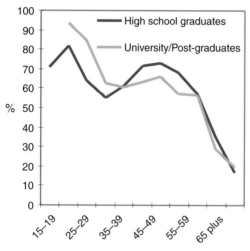

Figure 7.3 Female labour participation
(Adapted from Ministry of Labour *White Paper* 2000: 120, 133.)

Information and communications technologies

Contrary to popular wisdom, Japan is neither at the forefront of ICT penetration nor its cutting-edge applications. In fact, until the mid-1990s, the use of personal computers was not at all widespread. Accordingly, growth, while rapid, starts from a quite low base. It was not until June 1995 that the number of Japanese Internet users topped the one million mark. According to the *2000 Communications White Paper* (Ministry of Posts and Communications 2000), the number of

Internet access points increased 20-fold in Japan between 1996 and 2000. According to IDC Japan, mobile computing remains central to the domestic computer market with the sustained boom in mobile phones (cell and PHS (Personal Handy-phone system), year-on-year growth of some 20 per cent to total 56.2 million in fiscal year 1999) and high sales of portable computers (4.72 million sales in 1999 or 153.9 per cent year-on-year growth). In fact, for 3 years running, portable computers have accounted for more than 40 per cent of sales in the domestic market, twice the worldwide average (IDC Japan 2000).

As in other advanced economies, this steady diffusion of ICT has contributed to growing corporate interest in the business/management implications of the 'Information Age', as has the prolonged economic recession and increasingly robust global competition.

Current penetration of flexible work arrangements in Japan

While the innovative nature of Japanese management practices in the manufacturing sector is relatively well documented both inside and outside Japan, the same situation does not immediately apply to the services/information sector, which has accounted for the majority of Japanese workers since 1995. In fact, the Japanese office environment is essentially a conservative one with many in-built structural and market rigidities.

The well-known lifetime employment system, seniority-based pay and in-house unions have characterised the rise of post-war corporate Japan, especially since the boom years of the 1960s. Despite the fact that only a minority of the labour force, namely the salaried employees of large firms, enjoyed this strong job security, the existence of the system has had a far-reaching impact on the structure of the labour market, labour fluidity and hiring practices in particular. While much lip service is paid to the need for greater flexibility in the white-collar workplace, the Japanese office is still entrenched in conventional work patterns, as the following synopsis shows.

For example, such well accepted work arrangements in other industrialised countries, as compressed workweeks or job-sharing, are seemingly non-existent in Japan. The most commonly found departure from conventional work patterns is flexitime, but even this is not widely established (see Table 7.1). While part-time work does exist, it is usually confined to university students, and so-called part-time work for more mature workers is often a euphemism for full-time work without the benefits enjoyed by a long-term employee. This latter form of part-time work resembles the French CDD (contract of determinate duration), as opposed to the CDI (contract of indeterminate duration).

Other work options, including a discretionary work system (workers in certain designated occupations and their employers are exempt from the legal obligation to report the number of hours worked) and home-based work are very much the exception rather than the rule. In short, flexible work arrangements are by no means well established in corporate Japan (see Table 7.2).

Conventional organisational practices in Japan

Despite the relatively large-scale adoption of flexible work arrangements in other advanced economies, the fact that such work styles are less evident in the Japanese workplace needs to be investigated. To this end, it is useful first to consider the nature of conventional organisational practices in Japanese organisations.

Post-war Japanese corporations have been characterised by the 'holy trinity' of long-term (lifetime) employment, seniority-based pay systems, and company unions (see, for example, Ableggen 1958; Ihara 1999). These three

Table 7.1 Percentage of Japanese firms with flexible time arrangements

	All arrangements	Annual flexihours	Monthly flexihours	Flexitime
1988	7.0	*0.1	6.0	0.8
1994	27.4	*1.6	22.7	3.9
1995	30.1	8.7	18.3	4.3
1996	40.5	15.1	22.4	4.8
1997	54.4	35.9	16.3	4.4
1998	54.8	34.3	17.5	5.1

*Figures represent quarterly periods (April 1994 Amendment of the Labour Standards Legislation extended maximum flexihour calculation periods from 3 months to 1 year).

Source: *1999 Overall Survey on Wages/Work Hours*, Ministry of Labour.

Table 7.2 Percentage of workers by work arrangements

Options	All industries	300 plus	100–299	50–99	30–49
Shift work	25.4	23.5	26.3	24.5	27.4
Staggered days off	35.6	31.1	35.6	38.9	36.2
Flexible work hours:					
Annual/monthly/weekly	9.2	7.9	10.6	9.8	7.4
Flexitime	7.0	15.0	3.6	5.5	5.3
Discretionary work system	2.9	2.9	2.7	2.8	3.3
Off-site work system	1.9	2.0	2.0	1.4	2.2
Staggered work hours	9.4	9.9	10.2	9.0	7.9
Home-based work	0.2	0.1	0.3	0.2	0.1
Child-care leave	1.8	2.0	2.0	1.8	1.3
Elder-care leave	0.3	0.5	0.2	0.2	0.3
Refresh leave	8.3	16.6	7.1	5.6	4.3
Community service leave	0.2	0.3	0.1	0.1	0.3

Source: *1998 Service Industry Survey*, Ministry of Labour (June 1999).

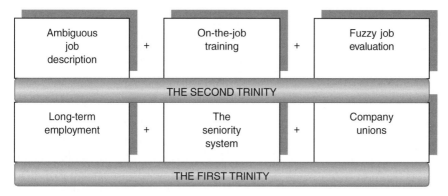

Figure 7.4 Japanese organisational trinities

systemic features have quite clearly played a dominant role in determining the nature of organisational behaviour in the Japanese corporate context. While economic upheaval in the past decade has started to erode some of these entrenched practices, the premise of long-term employment and seniority systems still exercises a significant impact on work design and work perform-ance in Japanese companies. This is especially true regarding a second 'trinity' of Japanese organisational characteristics: ambiguous job descriptions, on-the-job training and 'fuzzy' job performance evaluation (see Figure 7.4).

Job descriptions

Needless to say, attitudes toward job descriptions impact upon all organisa-tional functions, from hiring methods to pay systems, training, promotion and evaluation. It is by now a well established fact that individual job descriptions are extremely vague in the Japanese company (Iida 1998; Yashiro 2000). The pertinent question here, however, is not why job descriptions are vague, but why have Japanese companies been able to function in the absence of clear-cut job definitions? One argument posited by Miyamoto (1999) is that the concept of a specific job post (*shokumu*) has not been important for Japanese com-panies. The key concept in Japanese organisations has been, and remains, 'job (functional) status' (*shokuno*). Under this system, the status of an individual worker is clearly defined, but not the respective work brief (Lorriman and Kenjo 1996). Job status here does not refer to contractual or hierarchical status, but to the assumed degree of ability or functions required in a specific post (the literal translation of *shokuno* is job (*shoku*) and ability (*no*)). As long as the assumed degree of ability or function required is similar, workers in completely different areas performing very different jobs will share the same job status (and pay) (see Table 7.3).

Table 7.3 Conceptual differences between job, status and rank systems

Job system (*shokumu*)	Job content and extent of responsibility clearly defined
Status system (*shokuno*)	Individual's 'status' in the organisation clearly defined
Rank system (*shokui*)	Actual hierarchical ranking clearly defined

Adapted from Miyamoto (1999).

As has been pointed out elsewhere, the predominance of the status system has a far-reaching impact on pay and performance evaluation (Yashiro 2000). Miyamoto (1999) goes so far as to say that it divorces both pay and evaluation systems from the actual work performed. In other words, irrespective of differences in job types and individual posts, it is employee potential that is evaluated and ranked. And it is on this basis that pay and promotion are determined. This interpretation is borne out by the fact that despite the emergence of performance-related pay schemes in Japan in the 1990s, their share in total remuneration packages is far outweighed by the seniority-dominated 'basic wage portion' (*kihon-kyu*), which comprises a 'living portion' (*seikatsu-kyu*) and a 'status portion' (*shokuno-kyu*) (Figure 7.5). Moreover, the percentage of companies that have adopted some form of performance-based pay, while increasing, is still extremely low at 12.3 per cent (Figure 7.6).

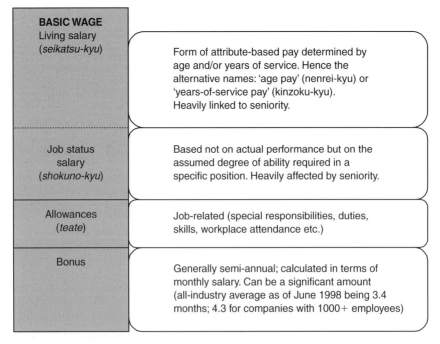

Figure 7.5 Typical composition of Japanese salaries

Adapted from Imano (1996: 118–24).

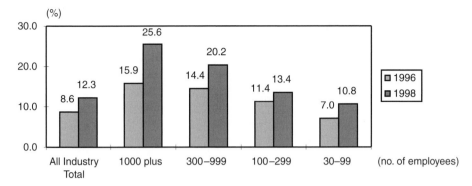

Figure 7.6 Japanese companies with performance-based pay (*nenpo-sei*)

Source: *JFY1998 General Survey on Wages and Working Hours System*, Japanese Ministry of Labour (1999c).

The weak emphasis on individual job descriptions and the overall tendency to bundle jobs at the team or small-group level mean that the group takes precedence over the individual (Iida 1998). This fosters a co-operative spirit as well as engendering a high sense of belonging, but naturally limits individual autonomy. The organisational advantages of such an arrangement are obvious, especially the resultant degree of staffing flexibility (Yashiro 2000). Tanaka (1988) points out that individuals, who could normally be expected to demand greater personal skill development and individual career opportunities, have also subscribed to this system because they were prepared to sacrifice personal development for stable, long-term employment. It remains to be seen, however, whether individual workers will be prepared to support this system as the Japanese business environment changes and long-term employment is no longer a given.

To sum up, individual job descriptions in Japanese organisations are highly ambiguous and are superseded by the concept of job status. The status system divorces pay and evaluation from the actual work performed. As will be seen in the next section, the predominance of the status system also impacts on conventional training practices in the Japanese organisation.

Skill formation

It is a well-documented fact that skill formation in Japanese companies relies quite heavily on on-the-job training (OJT) (Dore and Sako 1998; Iida 1998; McMurrer and Van Buren 1999; Ohta 1996) (see Figure 7.7). Needless to say, this is premised on the backbone of Japanese-style management: long-term employment within a single organisation and the resultant dependence on internal labour markets. A key aspect of the OJT system is that it is coupled

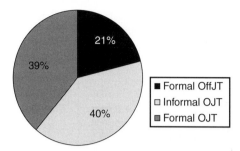

Figure 7.7 Distribution of employee learning
Source: McMurrer and Van Buren (1999)

with regular job rotation, facilitated by the previously discussed lack of specific job descriptions. It should be noted that the job rotation prevalent in Japanese office settings is inherently different to that put forward in the early 1920s as an antidote to job simplification (Parker and Wall 1998). Its focus is on career development rather than relieving physical or mental fatigue.

Simply stated, the type of training and skill formation that takes place under OJT is of a corporate-specific nature (Ohta 1996). While OJT has the advantage of not disrupting, but taking place simultaneously alongside, work, it does pose certain problems. For example, because of its informal nature—actual training is performed by individuals who themselves have been rotated through a series of different posts—it is extremely difficult to guarantee quality control. Additionally, affecting any change in training content takes considerable time.

There is a growing realisation, however, that specialist areas, like IT systems management and sophisticated financial product development, are ill-suited to OJT alone. Miyamoto (1999: 124) states that 'in areas where information technology plays a central role, the production efficiency generated by OJT-based skill formation and processes, a cornerstone of Japanese firms' competitive advantage, will no longer be an advantage'. Nevertheless, OJT and job rotation still form the nucleus of Japanese skill formation in the corporate context (Ministry of Labour 1999a).

Worker evaluation

Worker evaluation is perhaps the most crucial of all organisational features. Its ultimate goal is to assess the individual contribution of actors within the organisation. If, however, as we have seen, individual job descriptions and areas of responsibility are ambiguous, it is extremely difficult to verify the actual extent of contribution (Ohta 1996). This is the single greatest dilemma involved in appraising Japanese human resources performance.

Under the *shokuno* (status) system outlined above, different types of both latent and actual worker abilities are subject to evaluation. In addition to the ability to perform a specific job, attitude to work, level of motivation, co-operation with colleagues and the degree to which corporate objectives are understood are also taken into consideration (Miyamoto 1999). Most frequently, the results of this evaluation are expressed in the form of promotion; this means that workers are deeply interested in and affected by their evaluation by direct supervisors (Ohta 1996).

Ohta makes a further point:

> ...not only are evaluation standards extremely ambiguous in Japanese companies, more often than not the person doing the evaluation has received no training on how to evaluate. Since it is not possible to accurately evaluate in any objective manner the degree of contribution or ability, it is easy for the evaluation process to become one of parcelling out demerit marks.
>
> (Ohta 1996: 93)

As with skill formation, the limitations of this evaluation style have been raised, especially in connection with more specialist areas such as software programming. Miyamoto (1999: 124) states that 'in order to stimulate individual creativity, it is desirable that actual results are evaluated rather than ability and experience'. Nevertheless, the status quo is that results-oriented evaluation accounts for only a small part of worker evaluation in Japanese companies; that is, it hinges on assumed worker ability, is multifarious and tends towards marking down rather than marking up (*genten shugi*). As has already been discussed and illustrated in Figure 7.5, the predominance of seniority pay makes it possible, by and large, to divorce actual performance from financial reward, thereby making this 'fuzzy' system of evaluation tenable.

Implications of the Second Trinity

If we accept the premise that implementing a flexible work arrangement, such as telework, represents a reconfiguration of task characteristics, work roles and responsibility, as well as interaction with other members of the corporation, it is immediately apparent that the Second Trinity outlined above represents a major stumbling block, not only in terms of job, training and evaluation content, but in terms of the implementation of change.

Turning first to content, as has already been outlined, the existing combination of group-based jobs, frequent job rotation and broad-based OJT, culminates in 'fuzzy' evaluation where pay is divorced from actual performance. The absence of clearly delineated individual work portfolios and areas of responsibility contravenes both general work design principles and specific telework best-practice recommendations. Moreover, if job description ambiguity is intentional on the part of the organisation (as Iida (1998), for one, posits) it can be assumed that the resultant workplace culture will inhibit the engendering of individual work autonomy or task discretion, a key requisite for successful telework. It seems reasonable to assume, therefore, that as long as the job status (*shokuno*) system forms the backbone of Japanese HRM, the large-scale, effective adoption of telework, or indeed other flexible work arrangements, will be unlikely.

On the training front, the predominance of OJT is equally problematic because, at least in its present form, OJT assumes a) the presence of a long-term stable employment relationship between company and worker; and b) the sustained existence of a shared physical space. More critically, OJT implies an absence of formal training techniques, Shozugawa and Spinks (1999) go so far as to claim that a one-sided reliance on OJT is, in fact, tantamount to renouncing in-house education. While this view may be overstated, it is clear that the combination of informal training with frequent job rotation almost certainly opens up skill formation to a serious degree of random drift. Needless to say, traditional OJT practices have a poor fit with telework in the field. More crucially, however, OJT cannot respond at all to the content-specific and time-sensitive training needs of a work redesign program, for example, and certainly not for the implementation of a telework program.

Regarding evaluation, the consideration of a) latent ability, b) cooperation in the workplace, and c) attitude, relegates actual performance to the back seat and places the regular off-site worker at a distinct disadvantage. Ohta (1996) sees changes in work arrangements as being fundamentally unsuited to evaluating work attitudes, while Miyamoto (1999) states that the pursuit of performance-based evaluation is nothing less than a denial of both the seniority and *shokuno* systems. Ohta (1996) analyses the paradoxical relationship between existing evaluation systems and more autonomous work forms as follows:

> As long as existing human resource systems remain unchanged, there is a fear that [the introduction of more discretionary work arrangements] will only strengthen individuals' psychological sense of being fettered. . . . Might not the fact that very few people energetically exercise the option to work from home be attributable to the fact that HRM frameworks, including appraisal systems, do not cater to these new work arrangements?
>
> (Ohta 1996: 58)

Turning briefly to issues of process, it is clear that an appropriate and well established methodology for implementing change is generally lacking in the Japanese office work context. The organisational and intentional nurturing of ambiguity *per se* would seem to preclude the development of clear methodology. Reliance on OJT further obstructs a systematised approach to instilling new ideas, approaches and practices. And finally, 'fuzzy' evaluation precludes the need for rigorous discipline in that domain. As a result, the so-called Second Trinity not only impacts negatively on workplace practice from a work design perspective, it also hampers the development of an organisational framework for implementing swift and far-ranging change. Shifting workers through a series of different jobs is the only channel for effecting change, widening the skill base or fostering career development.

In this sense, the role of Japanese in-house human resource departments is crucial in dampening friction between established and new practices. Usually in charge of drawing up hiring plans, keeping individual worker records, mapping out career paths, liasing with the company union, keeping abreast of changes in labour legislation etc., these in-house departments have tended to act as conservative guardians of a highly stable and 'captive' workforce. Their importance in tailoring existing systems to fit better with new work arrangements (from mobile work to elder-care programmes), and providing the operational vocabulary for a new class of employees, cannot be overemphasised, as even Japanese companies begin to cut back their long-term employment commitments in favour of leaner and meaner employee relationships. Nor is their role negligible in making the changes that large-scale work redesign or telework require. Such efforts will mean the virtual reordering of the relationship between job descriptions, training, career development (=job rotation) and evaluation (see Figure 7.8).

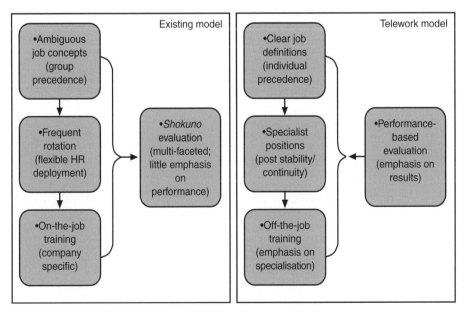

Figure 7.8 Existing and telework models

This is especially true when considering the result of the research by Bond *et al.* (1998), namely that job quality and workplace support are far more important predictors of workplace outcomes—including job satisfaction, commitment, loyalty to the employer, job performance and retention. This study identified determinants of job quality as: autonomy on the job, learning opportunities, meaningfulness of work, opportunities for advancement, and job security. Determinants of workplace support were identified as: flexibility in work arrangements, supervisor support, supportive workplace culture, positive co-worker relations, absence of discrimination, respect in the workplace, and equal opportunity for workers of all backgrounds.

Looking first at job quality, the fact that traditional job security and opportunities for advancement are being curtailed, as Japanese companies distance themselves from the seniority-based lifetime employment system, means remaining factors such as job autonomy, (formal) learning opportunities (of non-corporate specific skills) and meaningfulness of work (or task identity/significance, in the language of Hackman and Oldham) will need to be boosted. The results documented in Bond *et al.* (1998) would imply that without this, companies run the risk of poor organisational outcomes. Interestingly, a recent study on professional contract workers in Tokyo also found meaningfulness of work to be a stronger motivator than pay or job security (Metropolitan Tokyo Labour Research Institute 2000).

Regarding workplace support, the first three variables of flexibility in work arrangements, supervisor support and supportive workplace culture would seem to be the most urgent items to be addressed in the Japanese workplace, although the predicted diversification of worker demographics, including more female and senior workers, can be expected to strain the remaining variables in the not too distant future.[1]

Shifting the onus from the individual to the organisation

The importance of appropriate human resource systems when implementing flexible work arrangements is intuitively obvious. Such arrangements imply a more sophisticated approach to designing and managing human resource systems, a need raised in a recent ILO working paper highlighting the role of internal management consultants (IMC) (Prokopenko *et al.* 2000). Internal or in-house management consulting is depicted as a powerful instrument for enterprise restructuring, and 'an excellent across-the-board integrative mechanism to streamline enterprise efforts around the main strategic objectives' (ibid: Foreword). IMCs are viewed as 'change agents' and much more highly evolved than the often poorly managed personnel departments of yesteryear, which frequently failed to provide value to their host organisations (see, for example, Argyris 2000). In particular, Prokopenko *et al.* (2000 Ch. 1:

1.4) see 'a vital and valuable place for professionally run entrepreneurial and change-leading' internal consulting groups.

With many Japanese firms still mired in an industrial era mentality, top management tends to pay only lip-service to the importance of workplace leadership, while empowerment very rarely makes it to the agenda; yet these are precisely the facets that need to be stressed in order to respond to labour market and business changes. Positioning traditional HRM departments as internal management consultants, rather than guardians of the status quo, would go a long way in establishing a pragmatic mental and action platform for workplace transformation. As such, IMC is an area corporate Japan needs to examine.

As Figure 7.8 illustrates, the changes required to facilitate greater autonomy in the workplace, and by extension telework, are by no means insignificant (see Limburg's Chapter 6 for a detailed discussion on depth of organisational change). This virtual reordering of systemic priorities clearly falls within the parameters of organisational and/or work redesign. As such, there are natural limits to what a gifted worker and sympathetic supervisor alone can achieve. Nevertheless, it is not unusual even in well planned and supported telework programs for the onus of accommodating existing work practices into a new work arrangement to be placed on the individual teleworkers or the teleworkers/supervisor pairing. Various case studies show that it is possible for certain individuals to be successful at telework even in the absence of organisational support. Nevertheless, they remain the exception rather than the rule and represent a poor foundation for an exercise in work style change. As such, the onus for implementing change in work practices must lie firmly with the organisation, not the individual or individual supervisor/subordinate pairs.

A Third Trinity?

Much anecdotal and statistical evidence points to growing change in the traditional employee-workplace relationship in Japanese firms (see, for example, Mroczkowski and Hanaoka 1998; Sugiura 1997; Yashiro 2000). A marked jump in the rate of employee turnover for young workers has been noted (Ministry of Labour 1999a); fully 74.3 per cent of companies made mid-career hires in 1997–9 (Ministry of Labour 2000c); performance-based pay is making slow but steady inroads (see Figure 7.6); more companies are experimenting with new work arrangements (see, for example, Japanese case studies in ECaTT 1999); and remuneration and/or evaluation schemes are being revamped.

Moreover, as Yashiro (2000) points out, changes such as moving away from group-oriented work styles to evaluating the performance of clearly defined individual work units will be required of employers, irrespective of whether they are contemplating introducing a telework programme or not. In short, the case can be made that Japanese management, especially in the white-collar domain, is headed in the direction of a 'third trinity'. This, however, implies a radical overhaul of the founding premises of the so-called Japanese management system (Figure 7.9). Whether such a transformation will be widespread or confined to a small group of Japanese companies remains to be seen, but in order to take advantage of flexible work arrangements, some, if not all, of these changes will be inevitable.

It is intriguing to note that this Japanese call for clearly defined individual work briefs comes at a time when the trend for fostering greater teamwork moves forward in other advanced economies. Perhaps this is merely a reflection of differences in conventional management premises. In other words, Western organisations have to date focused systemically on the individual, as evidenced by extremely detailed job descriptions, individual performance indicators and highly differentiated remuneration according to individual post and performance. The Japanese context, as outlined above, approaches from the other end of the spectrum. So perhaps the new Japanese interest in clearer delineation and the Western focus on blurring individual/group lines represents a partial convergence of different organisational cultures. In other words, Rudyard Kipling may be wrong and the organisational twain can, indeed, meet.

Conclusions

This chapter has presented an outline of widespread Japanese work practices (the Second Trinity) that dovetail with the better known First Trinity of long-term employment, the seniority system and company union, and posits that the Second Trinity is a major stumbling block for implementing organisational change. Finally, it was suggested that the successful implementation of telework in a corporate context required shifting the focus of job bundling and work design from the individual worker to a more comprehensive organisational level. This implies the adoption of a work redesign approach, which, in turn, suggests that in-house HRM needs to evolve into in-house management consultants acting as agents of change, not opponents to change. In order to respond to this challenge, as well as to meet changes in the overall business environment, it was argued that nothing less than a shift to a Third Trinity would be required, with far-reaching implications for the traditional Japanese management system.

However, the speed at which such realignment may take place is unclear. Bearing in mind the size of sunken costs, especially administrative costs, in the traditionally very stable Japanese employment environment and the high degree of institutionalisation, the constraints on rapid structural change are by

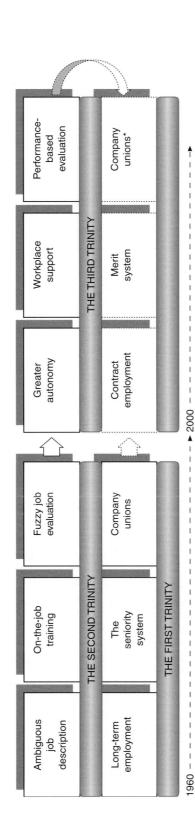

*encompassing contingent employees as well as traditional full-time employees

Figure 7.9 A new Japanese organisational trinity?

no means insignificant. This does not mean that change will not take place, but rather that it may occur in a drawn-out, cumulative manner, a pattern in keeping with past examples of organisational change in Japan. This is especially so given that a shift to flexible work arrangements like telework encompasses more political/personnel issues than technical issues, impinging, therefore, on an area where structural embedding mechanisms are often more unconscious than conscious (Schein 1992).

A final point is that, although this paper has anchored its arguments firmly in the Japanese organisational context, the issue of organisational legacies is not confined to that business culture alone. As other Chapters in this volume suggest, organisational views of reality (Järvinen, Chapter 10), the central concept of workplace (Gomes *et al.*, Chapter 4), physical workspace constructs (van der Linden, Chapter 5) and organisational learning (Limburg) are all affected, and often hampered, by structural and conceptual embeddedness. As such, the question of structural legacies is a pertinent one for all organisations that embark on a course of change.

Note

1 One may query the validity of extrapolating findings from US workplace research in toto to the Japanese workplace, but work by Japanese researchers cited in this paper such as Ohta, Sugiura and Yashiro, and others, including reports by the Japanese Ministry of Labour, depict the overall direction of Japanese employer-employee relations as resembling that described in Bond *et al.* (1998).

References

Ableggen, J.C. (1958) *The Japanese Factory: aspects of a social organization*, Glencoe IL: Free Press.
Argyris, C. (2000) *Flawed Advice and the Management Trap: how managers can know when they're getting good advice and when they're not*, New York: Oxford University Press.
Bond, J.T., Galinsky, E. and Swanberg, J.E. (1998) *The 1997 National Study of the Changing Workforce*, New York: Families and Work Institute.
Donaldson, L. (1995) *American Anti-management Theories of Organization: a critique of paradigm proliferation*, Cambridge Studies in Management 25, Cambridge: Cambridge University Press.
Dore, R. and Sako, M. (1998) *How the Japanese Learn to Work*, second edn, London: Routledge.
ECaTT (1999) 'New ways of work case studies—Japan', *Electronic Commerce and Telework Trends: Benchmarking Progress on New Ways of Working and New Forms of Business across Europe*, European Commission ESPRIT and ACTS programmes, Empirica: Bonn. (http://www.empirica.com/ecatt/).
Hannan, M.T. and Freeman, J. (1989) *Organizational Ecology*, Cambridge, MA: Harvard University Press.

IDC Japan (2000) Domestic PC shipments in 1999, press release, February 22: Tokyo. http://www.idcjapan.co.jp/Press/Current/20000222Apr.html.

Ihara H. (1999) *Text Management* (in Japanese), Minerva Text Library, Tokyo: Minerva Shobo.

Iida F. (1998) *A Critique of Japanese-style Management* (in Japanese), Tokyo: PHP Shinsho.

Imano K. (1996) *An Introduction to Human Resource Management* (in Japanese), Tokyo: Nihon Keizai Shinbunsha.

Lorriman, J. and Kenjo, T. (1996) *Japan's Winning Margins: management, training, and education*, Oxford: Oxford University Press.

McMurrer, D.P. and Van Buren, M.E. (1999) 'The Japanese training scene', *Training and Development*, 53, 8: 42–6.

Metropolitan Tokyo Labour Research Institute (2000) *Report on Peripheral Worker Categories and Labour Relations*, July, Tokyo.

Ministry of Labour (1999a) *White Paper on Labour 1999*, Japanese Government Publications: Tokyo.

—— (1999b) *1998 Service Industry Survey*, Japanese Government Publications: Tokyo.

—— (1999c) *1998 General Survey on Wages and Working Hours System*, Japanese Government Publications: Tokyo.

—— (2000a) *1999 Overall Survey on Wages/Work Hours*, Japanese Government Publications: Tokyo.

—— (2000b) *White Paper on Labour 2000*, Japanese Government Publications: Tokyo.

—— (2000c) *Survey on the Diversification of Hiring Strategies*, June 23, Japanese Government Publications: Tokyo.

Ministry of Posts and Telecommunications (2000) *2000 Communications White Paper*, Japanese Government Publications: Tokyo.

Miyamoto, M. (1999) *How to Protect Japanese Employment: where is the Japanese job status system headed?* (in Japanese), Tokyo: PHP Institute.

Ohta, H. (1996) *Organisational Theory that Respects the Individual: a new relationship between companies and the individual* (in Japanese), Tokyo: Chuko Shinsho.

Parker, S. and Wall, T. (1998) *Job and Work Design: organizing work to promote well-being and effectiveness*, Advanced Topics of Organizational Behavior, London: SAGE Publications.

Prokopenko, J., Johri, H. and Cooper, C. (2000) 'Internal Management Consulting: building in-house competencies for sustainable improvements', Enterprise and Management Development Working Paper, EMD/20/E, Geneva: ILO.

Schein, E.H. (1992) *Organizational Culture and Leadership*, second edn, San Francisco: Jossey-Bass Publishers.

Shouzugawa, Y. and Spinks, W.A. (1999) *An Introduction to Corporate Telework* (in Japanese), Tokyo: Nihon Keizai Shinbunsha.

Sugiura, Y. (1997) 'Study on a new trend of Japanese employment system' (in Japanese), *Monthly Labour Statistics and Research Bulletin*, 49, 5: 6–15, Tokyo: Ministry of Labour.

Tanaka, H. (1988) *Human Resource Management under Japanese-style Management* (in Japanese), Tokyo: Dobunkan.

Yashiro, N. (2000) 'Changing personnel management under flexible employment system' (in Japanese), *Japan Journal of Human Resource Management*, 2, 1: 2–9.

Part 4

Rethinking knowledge networking and virtual collaboration

This final part looks at both conceptual and practical developments in work innovations intended to overcome spatial and organisational constraints. In Chapter 8 by Nic Beech, George Cairns and Gerry Kincaid, the focus is on the role of ICTs in supporting learning across physical and social barriers. The authors seek to overcome the common dichotomies in approaches to knowledge management, such as between tacit and explicit, and individual and shared knowledge. They note that while much attention has been paid to the psychological context of knowledge and meaning generation, little consideration has been given to the *physical* learning setting. They note, moreover, that a general split has occurred in the management literature between discussion of the social and physical environments of work. One consequence of this has been an under-assessment of the role that workplace design plays in terms of the generation and dissemination of knowledge.

The authors seek to overcome these dichotomies by considering the 'psycho-physiology' of knowledge generation, dissemination and management through a case study of CELT, a general medical practitioner tool that supports self-directed learning. They illustrate the way the tool addresses a number of design issues that transcend traditional physical and knowledge management boundaries and discuss the way it helps to formalise certain learning processes. They also analyse issues related to the emotional aspects of learning and knowledge-generation, and link this to an understanding of 'private versus public' learning encounters.

The authors conclude that support for knowledge management processes must address both rational and emotional aspects of learning and take account of psychological as well as physical aspects of learning processes. A supporting environment in all these areas is needed, with the aim being to transcend the key dichotomies that dominate debate and development of knowledge management and learning systems.

Chapter 9 by Birger Rapp and Pauline Ärlebäck investigates developments in videoconferences in Swedish companies. Videoconferences, they note, were one of the big promises of modern ICT for the future workplace. After 20 to

40 years of experience with them, we must now admit that they were at least not the panacea expected for group communication over distance.

In their chapter, Rapp and Ärlebäck study videoconferencing usage in four-teen big Swedish organisations. In such cases one might expect to see wide application of videoconferencing, given Sweden's strong position in telecom-munications, the innovativeness of local companies and the country's long dis-tances. The results show, however, that little videoconferencing is actually used, and when it is, focus tends to be on *intra*-firm communication. Reasons for low usage can be put down to bad user interfaces, unreliability of the media, and the poor reputation engendered by such experiences, even though quality may well have improved in recent years.

An important contribution is made in the chapter by introducing the reader to media richness theory. The richer the media, and the greater the amount of information it can carry, the more complex the communication that can be developed through it. Seen in this light, they note, videoconferences should actually be the richest media available after personal meetings.

The authors conclude by developing the hypothesis that videoconferences work best when they support the running of routine meetings. This may also explain why they are mainly used for intra-organisational communication. The authors argue that the 'premature' implementation of videoconferences might lead to a permanent rejection of the technology. Indeed, this might already have happened in many cases. It is therefore suggested that videoconferences should be first introduced after users have first got to know each other through personal meetings. Once these basic issues are in order, successful implemen-tation of videoconferencing is more likely, with the success of the technology being measured in the saving of time and effort it produces, particularly in terms of travel.

The book concludes with a chapter by Pertti Järvinen. He draws in this on his extensive and deep knowledge of research methodologies. Through use of examples, he shows how a series of research approaches can be utilised by researchers in eBusiness and new ways of working. Järvinen differentiates between 'reality-studying' and mathematical approaches. Mathematical approaches work on sets of symbols and do not need an absolute connection to 'reality'. However, more emphasis is placed in the chapter on approaches con-cerned with studying reality. These are divided into 'reality describing' and 'reality changing' approaches—some might call these descriptive and norm-ative modes.

In the reality-changing approaches, innovation takes centre-stage. This is well in line with our search for new working methods, with analysis paid to innovations at different levels. Järvinen notes that research on the utility of innovations focuses either on building innovations or evaluating them post-implementation. In theoretical approaches, which themselves are another object of research work, Järvinen argues that sound logic and an ability to describe reality are typically more important than utility value. Empirical studies, he shows, fall into two camps: theory-testing and theory-creating. In addition, empirical phenomena can also be grasped on a conceptual-analytical basis, which differ from the pure mathematical approaches because of their orientation towards reality.

The chapter reminds us that researchers and practitioners in the general field of eBusiness and virtual working must master a wide variety of research approaches, as well as being appraised of the fundamental methodologies and epistemologies that underpin their work. Järvinen's review of Mowshowitz's virtual organisation characteristics also reminds us of an important fact: virtuality and its application has already been a traditional research object for hard computer science for some time; but for modern technologies, it represents a central practical and conceptual development, manifested in a variety of ways. It is now the task of work and organisational researchers to make virtual and electronic work concepts widely used and accepted, as commonplace in organisational studies as they are in computer science and related fields.

8 Networked knowledge

Challenges for learning across physical and social barriers

Nic Beech, George Cairns and Gerry Kincaid

Dichotomised thinking in knowledge management

Knowledge management is often subjected to dichotomised thinking. For example, distinctions are made between tacit and explicit knowledge (Nonaka 1991), individual and shared knowledge (Moingean and Edmondson 1996), and codification and personalisation processes of knowledge management (Hansen *et al.* 1999). Underlying these conceptual distinctions is the established theory of Argyris and Schön (1974, 1978) on single loop ('the how'), and double loop, ('the why') of learning. Although Argyris and Schön (1974) were careful to avoid over-simple characterisations, a view of knowledge as content (information, facts and data) plus *optional* processes—such as the interactive and social elements of learning (Brockbank and McGill 1998)—has persisted in having an impact on practice, particularly where 'codification' and 'transfer' (Bassi 1997) are the foci. In this chapter we seek to challenge some of the dichotomised thinking around knowledge management and argue for a view which incorporates rationality and emotion, openness and secrecy, physicality and virtualness, and anticipation and reflection.

One focus within knowledge management has been on 'explicit' knowledge (Pitt 1998) which can be codified (Hansen *et al.* 1999) in order to produce, store and transmit 'packages' of knowledge which will be useable by people distributed through the organisation. The knowledge of individuals is documented and dispersed through a company-wide application of information and communications technologies (ICT) and a sharing of best practice/recorded expertise (Bassi 1997). In such systems knowledge is 'distilled' (Fulmer *et al.* 1998) for inclusion, typically, in a database. Such processes inevitably entail selection, and this privileges the conceptual framework of those doing the selection. The design and format of the database are also part of the selection/privileging dynamic.

In this approach, learning is conceived as solitary and self-driven (Antonacopoulou 2000). It is assumed that those using the system can read the content of the message/page, and thereby gain an understanding of whatever the issues are. However, this would constitute a theoretical mode of learning (Saljo 1982) which does not necessarily engage the learner at a 'deep level' (Marton 1975). Initially, knowledge as power is located in the experts (French and Raven 1959), who have the power to provide or withhold information. Here, knowledge originates within the realm of the 'expert' and may be conceived as granting expert power (French and Raven 1959) to those who hold it. Once information is encoded and transferred to the ICT system, universal access to this information may reduce the informational power of the experts. However, where only partial or dependent dissemination occurs, or is granted, the power of the expert may be retained and may become manifest in expressed conference of referent or legitimate power by those who gain limited access. Alternatively, it may be seen only in the administration of insidious control by those who retain the key to knowledge as meaning.

A second focus within knowledge management is on 'tacit' knowledge (Pitt 1998) which is perceived as more personalised, creative but subjective, and shareable through the person-to-person channels of communication. Some (e.g. Galagan 1997) would argue that, in practice, tacit knowledge evolves through the more subtle and unintended nuances of interaction, and hence is not straightforwardly transferable to database technology. One answer to this problem can be envisaged through interactive group-based or networked software (Bassi 1997). Others, however, (e.g. Hansen *et al.* 1999) would argue that ICT is less likely to contain the possibilities for sharing of such knowledge, and that conversation and dialogue are necessary.

Under this conception of knowledge generation, the focus is on reflection through interaction (Beech and Brockbank 1999), and on acting on the basis of reflective interaction (Revans 1980). This style of learning seeks a deeper level of impact than the theoretical mode may achieve, where the learners feel themselves to be the agents of learning (Marton 1975), and the social context of the learning provides both reinforcement and flexibility of learning mode (Reynolds 1997). From a Foucauldian perspective (Foucault 1980), power is not located in the hands of individual actors. Rather, it is seen in the processes through which knowledge is constructed, prioritised and put to use. Power is not conceived as negative and constraining, but rather as constructive, forming the relational networks through which knowledge is created and constantly recreated. At a basic level it is a question of what people are willing and able to communicate, to whom, and in what form.

Although this second approach is apparently distinct from the first, on closer examination the distinctions are less discrete. In order for sharing to occur, tacit knowledge must become explicit. In so doing, it must be encoded, and the form of the encoding both demands, and relies on, selection of 'the important' factors and outcomes. This formation may be led either by the individual critically reflecting (Pedler 1984) on their own experience, or through questioning by others (Revans 1980). Either way, the selection will reflect power in the choices of which questions to ask and what to reveal in answering them. In addition to these conscious processes, people's priorities and responses will reflect their culture, values and unquestioned assumptions (Schein 1993). Hence, selection, codification and power dynamics are still at play. In practice, even where knowledge is gathered in a less structured way, it is necessary to impose a structure in order to manage it. In the example cited by Fulmer *et al.* (1998), drawn from Hewlett-Packard, although initial gathering of individual representations of knowledge of past events and artefacts produced a 'mess of stuff' (Fulmer *et al.* 1998: 17), this was reduced and rationalised to the level of themes and stories; these were codified and circulated using a two-column format based on Argyris's model, with questions and commentaries generated centrally in the second column. This does maintain a degree of critical and creative engagement with the stories, but it does also entail reduction and selection by the organisation in order to render the product manageable. That which is not manageable or useful is edited out and ignored. Thus the processes of power/knowledge define what is, and what is not.

The theories of knowledge generation by the individual discussed above are dependent upon consideration of the psychological context of knowledge and meaning generation, i.e. the context of the human mind. There has, however, been little consideration of the physical context of learning. Tacit learning is a process dependent upon interaction (Beech and Brockbank 1999) which, prior to the development of ICT, implies a shared physical context of space and facilities, yet the physical environment has received little attention in the managerial literature. Interest in the physical environment of work has been constrained by the ubiquitous Hawthorne experiments (Pennock 1930), from which the primary conclusion was that social factors are far more important determinants of employee behaviour and productivity than physical factors. This key 'finding' came as a great surprise to the research team (Roethlisberger 1941) but has become the 'central and distinctive finding from which the fame and influence of the Hawthorne studies derive' (Carey 1967: 405). The separation of the physical and the social environments of work, with the social as primary area of study, has been the dominant model throughout the period, a split that was further reinforced by Herzberg's (1966) placing of the physical within the dichotomous framework of motivators/hygiene factors. Again, no contribution of the physical environment to development and learning is identified.

While the physical environment of work has been underplayed in terms of its relevance to the generation and dissemination of knowledge, Baldry *et al.* (1998: 181) posit that 'buildings are seen as structures of control: this is, after all, *why* lots of people are brought together under one roof' (italics in original). Here, buildings are seen as a means of exerting legitimate power (French and Raven 1959) over employees, of constraining their behaviour and, by implication, their knowledge development. Why, then, should the new physical environment of the ICT system be considered any differently? If ICT represents the physicality of explicit learning, then buildings and space represent the physicality of tacit learning; the context of human interaction. If buildings can be constraining of human behaviour, of tacit learning, then we should consider how ICT systems might also be constraining of explicit learning.

The dichotomisation of thinking that we identify in the literature raises a series of issues about the psycho-physiology of knowledge generation, dissemination and management. These are represented in Figure 8.1. The two approaches make different assumptions about the nature of knowledge and knowledge-generation. In the first approach, power is located in the expert and the system design (once it is extracted from experts). In the second, it is not only located in the individual, or the expert, but is more dispersed in that tacit knowledge may emerge to become explicit at unpredictable times, and in unpredictable places. The network of those interacting becomes the 'shared space' in which knowledge and power are played out. In the first approach learning is an individual process, whereas in the second it is basically interactive.

We have argued that the dichotomy may not be clear and absolute. We will seek to explore these issues by reflecting on the case of a system for knowledge generation and management amongst general medical practitioners.

CELT

The system which is the subject of this study is CELT (Computerised Evaluative Learning Tool). Its purpose is to support self-directed learning for general medical practitioners (GPs) in Scotland. CELT is not an expert system which seeks to direct diagnosis and treatment planning. Rather, the focus is on

Approach 1	Approach 2
Codified	Personalised
Reductive/selective	Subjective/unstructured
Controlled by the individual/expert	Controlled by the individual/network/not controlled
Database	Interactive software ←——→ interpersonal dialogue
Workplace design:	Workplace design:
– can be dispersed	– physical proximity
– focus on ICT	– either interactive ICT or little focus on ICT

Figure 8.1 Dichotomised approaches to knowledge management

responding to, and learning from, day-to-day events. The system incorporates structured and unstructured input, and reports facts, perceptions and emotions. When a GP has a learning need, typically triggered by an event, such as an interaction with a patient in which diagnosis was not straightforward, they can use the system to manage their learning. The GP enters a record of the event and their learning needs; the system prompts them to manage their learning. The data entry encapsulates subjective narrative, but also prompts the GP to adopt an action-focus through the use of particular verbs. The system is not limited to simple facts, but also acknowledges that there can be an emotional element to learning through enabling the GP to incorporate more holistic reflections. In addition, tick-box screens record structured elements of data. Figure 8.2 shows the entry screen into the system.

The main purpose—individual learning—is served through recording, action planning and monitoring. Having recorded the initial event, the GP is prompted to decide on learning activities. CELT structures the learning process. It relates to some of the principles of action learning (Revans 1980) in focusing on a specific event (or set of events) which are real and meaningful for the learner, prompting personal reflection through a combination of open expression and questioning, and subsequent action and 'report back'. Figure 8.3 shows a screen which prompts the GP into recording the learning need.

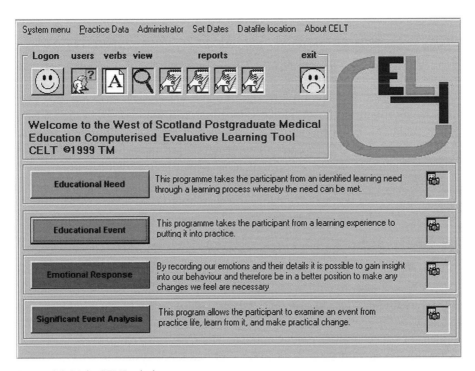

Figure 8.2 Main CELT splash screen

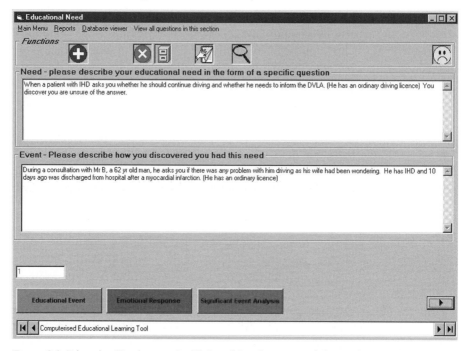

Figure 8.3 Education Need screen 1 of 5 describing the event and the resultant need

The motivation for becoming actively involved is twofold: the intrinsic motivation of learning and the extrinsic motivation of recording learning events and processes which score continuous professional development (CPD) points. GPs need to maintain a recognised amount of CPD activity each year in order to obtain the Postgraduate Education Allowance (PGEA), and CELT offers one way of achieving part of this requirement. They may plan to develop their knowledge by use of information put onto the system by other users, or they may devise learning actions which include getting information from other sources, such as the Internet, and formal training. A further development for CELT will be to enhance the searching facility and enable users to search a central database via the Web. The system can also be used proactively. For example, where a problem arises repeatedly, targeted courses and information could be made available to the professional network.

In addition, the system provides an audit function (see Figures 8.4 and 8.5). Currently it is self-driven, so that the GPs can track their own learning needs, actions and reflections over time. The profession is aware of potential increases in litigation by dissatisfied patients, and of the need of GPs to be able to give evidence of their proactive development. The CELT system provides one way of tracing the data for these needs. It is a 'closed loop' system in which, when a GP generates an event, they have to close it off by taking some action which

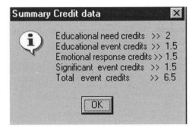

Figure 8.4 Credit summary dialog box

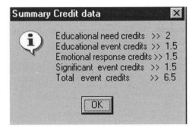

Figure 8.5 Education Need screen 2 of 5

they decide on, and reporting it. The system prompts the GP on any outstanding action points, so that they cannot be easily forgotten or ignored.

At present the system is distributed on CD upon request or as a download from the CELT website. The website download is based on a 42-day trial version with an access code available for a nominal fee. The website is being developed to facilitate online access to a central CELT database storing all anonymised CELT entries. Standard website functionality, such as discussion groups and newsgroups, are also being considered. In addition, users will be able to correspond with relevant GPs based on individual entries or experiences. These developments will enhance the possibilities for communal learning. The learning already has a communal element in that the data is generated by a community of practitioners, but further enabled interaction would diminish the physical boundaries to interactive learning of a professional group which is necessarily dispersed.

The system is designed to incur the least possible cost in terms of finance and time for the user. The system runs on entry-level business PCs running Windows 95/98/NT/2000. This system is standard in most practices.

The concept behind CELT is generic to any contact situation resulting in a learning need based on lack of specialist knowledge. A version of the system for dentists has been developed and is currently in beta test. Conceptually, the dental system is identical to the primary care system but with relevant examples and help files.

Discussion

No single system can enable best learning practice for all users. However, CELT does engage with a number of design issues that seek to cross some traditional boundaries in knowledge management, as well as those of physical space. It formalises learning through questioning/analysis, action planning and monitored report-back. Public self-analysis is enabled, and there is acknowledgment that learning and knowledge are not just about facts and information. The role of emotion has long been recognised by some in the field of human resource development (Hochschild 1983), despite some approaches such as the competency movement, which focused mainly on the behaviourally observable. Similarly, in the knowledge management and intellectual capital debates (Stewart 1997), in spite of some acknowledgment of emotionality, the focus has been on the observable. CELT seeks to acknowledge that learning and knowledge-generation are not emotion-free activities, and this is illustrated in Figure 8.6.

In a sense, opening up to one's peers can be a form of confession which can be highly invasive when done face-to-face (Beech *et al.* 2000). The advantages of openness in a group setting are the frequent realisation that one is not alone in having a particular problem and the emotions associated with it, and the possibility of gaining questioning and advice which lead to action. The disadvantage is that once something is confessed (a fear, a failure, a worry, etc.) it cannot be unconfessed. That knowledge becomes public, and can potentially be used as a source of power against the individual. One of the key advantages of ICT knowledge systems is that a supportive peer group can be enacted while anonymity is maintained. Thus, openness and confidentiality can be achieved.

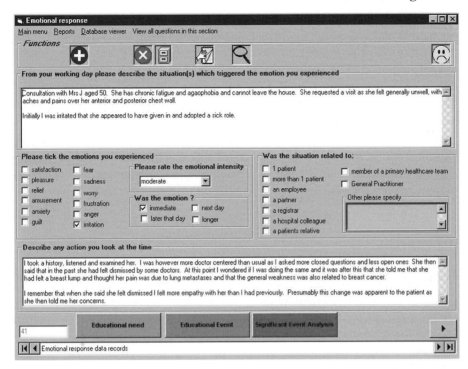

Figure 8.6 Emotional response form outlining the event and generated emotional response

Conclusions

The purpose of networked knowledge systems, such as CELT, is to provide learning and decision support, based on real rather than hypothetical events. In order to achieve this, we would argue that it is important to address certain dichotomies and, where possible, to escape from traditional 'either/or' forms of thinking. In particular, there is a need for individual analysis, action and collective learning between peers. Contributors need to be able to choose what they are going to be open about, and what they keep secret. Both rational analysis and planning, and emotional engagement are needed, and a balance has to be struck between the reductive/selective and the subjective/unstructured approach to knowledge management. The psycho-physiological environment of knowledge generation and dissemination must provide useability, functionality and emotional comfort to the user. That is to say that the psychological context of knowledge management must be supportive of the user's needs for expression of lack of knowledge and fear of failure—past and future—as well as of the positive aspects of knowledge acquisition. In support of the psychological context, the physical context must also be designed to suit the needs of the user. The ICT system must be user friendly, accessible and responsive on the user's terms. It must also enable the user to access and interact with it and with others within a supportive physical environment of their own choosing. The overall environment of operation and use is developing towards a post-dichotomous construct of physical location/freedom, proximity/remoteness, supported by ICT, that provides emotional security/openness. Thus, the operation of power needs to be both in individual choices and dispersed in the network.

While these are not the only lines of tension, we would argue that they present some of the significant challenges that must be borne in mind during the processes of problem definition, design, implementation and use of knowledge management systems.

References

Antonacopoulou, E.P. (2000) 'Employee development through self-development in three retail banks', *Personnel Review*, 29, 4: 491–508.

Argyris, C. and Schön, D. (1974) *Theory in Practice: increasing professional effectiveness*, London: Jossey-Bass.

—— (1978) *Organisational Learning: a theory of action perspective*, Reading, Mass.: Addison-Wesley.

Baldry, C., Bain, P. and Taylor, P. (1998) 'Bright satanic offices: intensification, control and team Taylorism', in P. Thompson and C. Warhurst (eds) *Workplaces of the Future*, Basingstoke: MacMillan Business.

Bassi, L.J. (1997) 'Harnessing the power of intellectual capital', *Training and Development*, 51, 12: 25–31.

Beech, N. and Brockbank, A. (1999) 'Power/knowledge and psychosocial dynamics in mentoring', *Management Learning*, 30, 1: 7–26.

Beech, N., Cairns, G. and Robertson, T. (2000) 'Transient transfusion; or the wearing-off of the governance of the soul', *Personnel Review*, 29, 4: 460–75.

Brockbank, A. and McGill, I. (1998) *Facilitating Reflective Learning in Higher Education*, Buckingham: Society for Research into Higher Education and Open University Press.

Carey, A. (1967) 'The Hawthorne studies: a radical criticism', *American Sociological Review*, 1967, 32: 403–16.

Foucault, M. (1980) *Power/Knowledge: selected interviews and other writings 1972–77*, Brighton: Harvester Press.

French, J.R.P. and Raven, B. (1959) 'The bases of social power', in D. Cartwright (ed.) *Studies in Social Power*, Michigan: Michigan Institute for Social Research.

Fulmer, R.M., Gibbs, P. and Keys, J.B. (1998) 'The second generation learning organisations: new tools for sustaining competitive advantage', *Organisational Dynamics*, 27, 2: 6–21.

Galagan, P. (1997) 'Smart companies', *Training and Development*, 51, 12: 20–35.

Hansen, M.T., Nohria, N. and Tierney, T. (1999) 'What's your strategy for managing knowledge?' *Harvard Business Review*, March–April: 102–20.

Herzberg, F. (1966) *Work and the Nature of Man*, New York: Staples Press.

Hochschild, A. (1983) *The Managed Heart*, Los Angeles: University of California Press.

Marton, F. (1975) 'What does it take to learn?' in N. Entwistle and D. Hounsell (eds) *How Students Learn*, Lancaster: Institute for Research and Development in Post-Compulsory Education.

Moingean, B. and Edmondson, A. (1996) *Organisational Learning and Competitive Advantage*, London: Sage.

Nonaka, I. (1991) 'The knowledge-creating company', *Harvard Business Review*, 69, 2: 96–104.

Pedler, M. (1984) 'Management self-development', in B. Taylor and H. Lippit (eds) *Handbook of Management Development*, London: McGraw Hill.

Pennock, G.A. (1930) 'Industrial research at Hawthorne', *Personnel Journal*, 8: 296–313.

Pitt, M.R. (1998) 'Strategic learning and knowledge management', *Human Relations*, 51, 4: 547–63.

Revans, R. (1980) *Action Learning: New Techniques for Action Learning*, London: Blond and Briggs.

Reynolds, M. (1997) 'Learning styles: a critique', *Management Learning*, 28, 2: 115–33.

Roethlisberger, F.J. (1941) *Management and Morale*, Cambridge: Harvard University Press.

Saljo, R. (1982) *Learning and Understanding: a study of differences in constructing meaning from a text*, Gothenburg: Acta Universitatis Gothenburgensis.

Schein, E. (1993) 'On dialogue, culture and organisational learning', *Organisation Dynamics*, 22, 2: 40–51.

Stewart, T. (1997) *Intellectual Capital*, New York: Doubleday.

9 An explorative study of videoconferencing in Swedish companies

Birger Rapp and Pauline Ärlebäck

Human beings have always used different means to communicate. The new information communication technology (ICT) challenges us to develop new working conditions and new organisational solutions. Spinks (Chapter 7) and van der Linden (Chapter 5), respectively, discuss virtual ways of working. In this context, communicating techniques become an important issue. Furthermore, Spinks and Limburg (Chapter 6) discuss teleworking. They, as well as Björkegren and Rapp (1999) and Rapp and Rapp (1999), stress the need for successful teleworkers to have good tools at their disposal in order to be able to communicate with others. In such circumstances the opportunity for videoconferencing becomes a possibility. This, then, will be the starting point for our discussion on issues relating to the design of collaborative environments. However, according to media richness theory (MRT), videoconferencing should by now be used widely. Is this in fact the case? In this chapter we will look at the use of videoconferencing more closely. Our investigation will focus on the use of videoconferencing in Sweden today and we will also try to find explanations for why the diffusion of this 40-year-old innovation has been slow in coming about. Our results will throw new light upon videoconferencing as a solution to some of the issues raised in this chapter, as well as in other chapters in this volume.

Our investigation is an explorative study and in it we have viewed fourteen companies, some of them among the largest in Sweden, with our focus on their use of videoconference meeting rooms. Based on interviews and literature, we have also formulated some hypotheses regarding how videoconferencing is used, the relationship between videoconferencing and other media and, finally, the implementation of videoconferencing.

Teleworking is not an easy task. It has to be approached seriously if people are to communicate with each other effectively. In this context videoconferencing is often regarded as a new way of communicating using ICT. But is videoconferencing a promising technique and are Swedish companies really starting to use it? We can initially state that the use of videoconferencing in different large Swedish companies is connected with the following questions:

- How is videoconferencing used?
- For what reasons is videoconferencing used?
- For what is videoconferencing a substitute?

Background

No major study has previously been conducted into the use of videoconferencing in large Swedish companies, even though the technique behind videoconferencing is an old one. But despite frequently repeated reports of how videoconferencing will replace face-to-face communication, very little has happened up until now; videoconferencing does not seem to be widely used in businesses.

We define 'videoconferencing' as communication between at least two parties,[1] using videoconference equipment in special studios. We will not study the use of desktop systems nor use the concept of 'video meeting'. In some studies the latter term is used instead of 'videoconference' (see Åbom 1997).

The aim of the study is to find out whether there has been an increase in the use of videoconferencing, and to examine how the technique is used. In addition, we formulate several hypotheses regarding the use of videoconferencing.

The next section gives a short frame of reference and justification of our approach. We will then report on the results of interviews with individuals who are responsible for the booking of videoconference studios. Finally, in the last section, we will raise a number of hypotheses about the use of videoconferencing, the relationship between videoconferencing and other media, and the implementation of videoconferencing.

Research strategy

The overall aim of this study is to gain an understanding of videoconferencing in Sweden, and to formulate hypotheses. The method used for these purposes is an explorative study. The companies studied were chosen from among the largest Swedish companies, in the belief that these companies will take full advantage of videoconference studios. This is also supported by, for example, Arnfalk (1999), who claims that videoconferencing is primary an internal communication aid. Thus, we can expect to find videoconferencing in large companies. We have selected companies on the basis of their 1999 sales, and have also included some IT companies. Furthermore Åbom (1997) has already conducted some studies of small Swedish companies.

To explore the use of videoconference studios, we conducted telephone interviews with the persons responsible for booking videoconference studios in fourteen Swedish companies. The questions were structured and were related to the following issues:

• Is videoconferencing used and, if so, how often?
• Who in the organisation uses videoconferencing?
• What is videoconferencing used for (internal/external, two parties or more, Swedish/international contacts, the task performed)?

We also interviewed some direct users of videoconference systems.

Frame of reference

A very general definition of communication is: 'You cannot not communicate'. This also means that your choice of medium itself may transmit different signals. Daft and Lengel (1984, 1986) elaborated on this and proposed the media richness theory (MRT). They argue that the richness of a medium is characterised by its ability to transmit signals that reduce ambiguity. In addition, media richness is related to a medium's ability to give feedback, to its ability to allow natural language and to transmit personal feelings, and to the possibilities it has of using different cues (Lengel and Daft 1988; Trevino *et al.* 1990). Face-to-face meetings, for example, are regarded as a rich medium and email as a low medium.

The literature discusses when and if it is possible to choose a medium related to the complexity of the task to be transmitted (see, for example, Egido 1990; Huber and Daft 1987; Rapp 1993; Sitkin *et al.* 1992; Sproull and Kiesler 1986). If effective communication is defined as communication where the effects obtained are equal to the intended effects, there exists a substitution effect between media. This is shown in Figure 9.1.

The MRT has been tested and there are both supporting and contradicting results (see, for example, Fulk and Steinfeld 1990; Fulk and Boyd 1991; Dennis and Kinney 1998). The theory has also been criticised by many authors for not considering relevant factors.

Many studies indicate that social influence is important for the use of both new and old media (see, for example, Fulk and Boyd 1991; Markus 1994; Sitkin *et al.* 1992; Webster and Trevino 1995; Yates and Orlikowski 1992). Sproull and Kiesler (1986) introduce three different social variables: geographical, organisational and situational. These situational variables are related to the specific communication situation, and depend on social cues. Obviously not all cues are the same for different media. Kydd and Ferry (1994) stress that there are differences of views regarding the richness of a medium, depending on whether the point of view is objective or subjective. Besides, two communicators need not share the same frame of reference (see, for example,

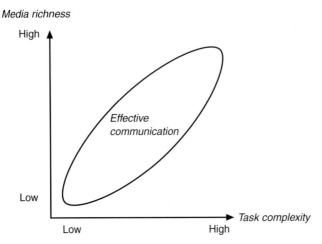

Figure 9.1 Effective communication
(Adapted from Daft and Lengel 1984: 199; Rapp 1993: 135).

Lindström 1999). The choice of medium, Yates and Orlikowski (1992) argue, is related to the group's perception of the medium and is not individually based. Traditions differ within the organisation (Maltz 2000).

Videoconferences and how they are used

Both Egido (1990) and Arnfalk (1999) suggest that videoconferencing is most suitable for internal use. They claim that this may change when the equipment has become more standardised. Campbell (1997, 1998), too, supports this argument. King and Weidong (1997) have found that a user's perception of different media changes with his or her knowledge and experience of these media.

An often-heard assertion is that videoconferencing will replace travel (for example, Carey 1996; Egido 1990; and Feldman 1993). Rapp and Skåmedal (1996) and Arnfalk (1999), for example, identify three situations: first, video-conferencing can replace the face-to-face meeting; second, it can be a comple-ment to face-to-face meetings in order to make it possible to communicate more frequently; finally, videoconferencing can also generate new meetings if the contacts through videoconferences create the need for further face-to-face meetings.

Videoconferencing and its relationship to other media

The face-to-face meeting is a richer medium than the videoconference. But the videoconference is a richer medium than the telephone conference. According to MRT, videoconferences should be able to replace some face-to-face meetings but also some telephone conferences. Some studies (see Fulk 1993; Karahanna and Straub 1999; Schmitz and Fulk 1991) show that users sometimes choose a richer medium than MRT indicates. They explain that this is due to the habits of the user. If the user has sent some messages with one medium, he or she will not change this medium in order to be more effective when it is time for the next message.

One argument against applying the MRT results to companies is that videoconferencing is a new technique and therefore cannot be directly compared with old media. However Rognes (1999) argues that in the long run, MRT will be valid. Dennis and Kinney (1998) however disagree with that argument.

Webster (1998) summarises some factors behind the individual choice of media and divides them into three groups: media choice factors, the acceptance of new technology in the organisation, and the privacy aspect. According to Åbom (1997), for example, the result of a videoconference will be better if those who are involved in the meeting have previously met face to face and have got to know each other.

Implementing videoconferences

Videoconference systems still represent a new technology. Hård and Jamison (1996) argue that the old structure within the organisation supports the retention of old techniques. They identify three levels: the symbolic level (including the attitudes and values associated with the new techniques), the organisational level, and the level of individual behaviour. Sturesson (2000), too, supports this view and argues that a new technique has difficulties in being accepted if the new technology is different from the old on all three of these levels.

Lindström (1996) and Markus (1990) stress that the value of the interactive system increases with the number of users. Thus the value of a new interactive medium is low as long as it has few users. At present, videoconferencing is mostly used by organisations as an internal medium and, thus, according to Egido (1990), the critical mass argument is not directly applicable. Furthermore, Johansson and Stenbacka (1995) point out that the acceptance of videoconference systems is dependent on standards, although a standard was not introduced until the 1990s. We can thus expect wider use of videoconferences in the future.

The two Swedish studies on videoconferencing, Åbom (1997) and Arnfalk (1999), report that users encounter technical problems when trying this technique.

Results of the survey

The results from interviews with those who were responsible for booking the video studios are summarised in Table 9.1. This shows that videoconferencing has grown significantly since 1995. One reason may be technical advances that have brought acceptable levels of sound and image quality. Technological progress has also reduced the cost of equipment and the cost of its use.

All but one of the companies that were interviewed had made investments in videoconference equipment and studios in the period after 1995. The exception is Company 12, which made its investment only a few months before the interview. This company therefore has little experience in the use of the medium.

It was not possible to draw any general conclusions from our study concerning who is using videoconferences or which departments the user works in. However, since companies look upon videoconferencing as a substitute for travel, the users of videoconferencing are all people with frequent contacts outside their own offices. Videoconferencing most often involves parties in different countries. Considering the potential savings in both time and money, this is to be expected.

The number of parties involved in a videoconference varies, but it is often between two and four. This is interesting since meetings with more than two parties are more technically complicated and costly, due to the need for Multipoint Control Units, which must be leased from an external provider.

We have found that videoconferencing is an intra-organisational phenomenon. The great majority of the videoconferences are regular internal meetings. However, in some cases there are also outside parties involved. These are primarily customers and/or suppliers. In some companies, videoconferencing was used two to four times a week. In others, it was one to three times a month. Only in three companies was videoconferencing used daily. In these three companies, however, there were international team groups, with members working in different countries.

Table 9.1 The general results of the study

	Has video conference equipment	User group	Frequency	Number of parties involved	Communication partners	Internal/External
Company 1	Yes	Not applicable (not from the lower hierarchy-levels)	3 times a week	Mostly 2, multipoint does occur	Sweden and abroad	Both
Company 2	Yes	Project groups	2–4 times a week	Mostly multipoint	Mostly abroad	Mostly internal, external occurs
Company 3	Yes	Not applicable	More than once a month	2	Mostly abroad	Internal
Company 4	Yes	Not applicable	Once a week	Mostly 2, multipoint does occur	Mostly abroad	Mostly internal, external occurs
Company 5	Yes	Not applicable	At least once a day	So far only possible with 2	Sweden and abroad	Internal
Company 6	Yes	Not applicable	2 times a month	Not applicable	Mostly abroad	Mostly internal, external occurs
Company 7	Yes	Not applicable	2–3 times a month (to increase?)	Both	Sweden and abroad	Above all internal
Company 8	Yes	Not applicable	5 times a day	Mostly 3–4 parties, everything between 2 and 6 parties does occur	Mostly abroad	Internal
Company 9	Yes	Managers and project groups	5–6 times a week	Mostly multipoint	Sweden	Internal
Company 10	Yes	Not applicable	3 times a week	Mostly 2	Mostly Sweden and USA	Internal
Company 11	Yes	Not applicable (frequent within project groups)	4–5 times a day	Mostly multipoint (on the average 5 parties)	Mostly abroad	Internal
Company 12	Yes (approx. one month)	Not applicable	Not applicable	Not applicable	Not applicable	Not applicable
Company 13	Yes	Not applicable	3 times a day	50% multipoint (3–4 parties)	90% abroad	Mostly internal, external occurs
Company 14	Yes	Not applicable	Not applicable	Mostly 2, multipoint does occur	Sweden and abroad	Mostly internal, external occurs

Discussion and hypothesis

We will now formulate our observations as hypotheses and, if possible, relate them to the literature we have mentioned.

The use of videoconferences

Many of the users stated that videoconferences were often follow-up meetings. Thus, the medium was primarily used for routine meetings that do not include any deep discussion. Campbell (1997) also supports this view.

> Hypothesis 1: Videoconferencing is mostly suitable for routine meetings

This hypothesis contradicts the results of applying the media richness theory, which states that videoconferencing should be used when there is a high degree of complexity and not for routine meetings. Videoconferencing, according to MRT, is a rich medium, exceeded in richness only by face-to-face meetings. However, videoconferencing is a new medium and, therefore, users are still not comfortable with it. Because of this, they do not fully understand its richness (see King and Weidong 1997).

   This study does not show clearly whether videoconferencing is mainly a tool for one-way communication or an interactive tool for two-way communication. About 50 per cent of the users claimed that videoconferencing is mainly used for information (one-way communication). The remaining users said that the communication is an interactive two-way communication. One explanation for these results could be that users have different habits regarding videoconferences. The technical conditions of videoconferences demand strict meeting discipline. Thus, if the participants are not used to videoconferencing, they can have difficulties in maintaining a dialogue; but this is necessary if they want to solve tasks with a high degree of complexity. We therefore suggest the following hypothesis:

> Hypothesis 2: With increased experience of videoconferencing, the possibility of successful dialogues increases and the use of videoconferences will be asymptotical, as MRT predicts

Videoconferencing in relation to other media

We also asked the respondents to compare videoconferencing with telephone conferences and face-to-face meetings. According to the MRT, videoconferences are richer than telephone conferences but less rich than face-to-face meetings.

In comparing telephone conferences with videoconferences, the respondents emphasised that video is a visual medium. This is helpful in discussions, where, for example, some of the conferencing parties speak a foreign language. As one of the respondents said, 'the visual impression of the speaker is a part of your interpretation.' All the comments that are related to the advantages of videoconferences are in line with MRT. Another important feature of a videoconference is the opportunity to display drawings or diagrams during the conference. This is even more important than being able to see the faces of the other party. This leads us to the following hypothesis:

> Hypothesis 3: Compared to a telephone conference, the visual aspect of video-conferencing—to be able to see the person to whom you are talking—is important, but even more important is the possibility of sharing documents and data

The most important advantages of a videoconference, as compared to a face-to-face meeting, are the time and cost aspects. The travel time eliminated allows more time to be devoted to effective work. The videoconferences are also efficient, since they require careful preparation. They also require a certain degree of meeting discipline. Furthermore, this medium does not encourage small talk, so meetings are more focused on the agenda; depending on the purpose of the meeting, this can be more or less appropriate. For instance, when team-building is an important aspect of a meeting, efficient communication is a minor consideration.

Videoconferencing is regarded as cost-effective due to savings made in time and travel costs. These savings, in turn, allow for more frequent contacts during the critical phases of a project. This leads to the following hypothesis:

> Hypothesis 4: When compared to a face-to-face meeting, the primary advantages of videoconferencing are those of time and cost efficiency

Videoconferences also have some disadvantages, but all the disadvantages mentioned by the respondents were only actualised when they compared the videoconference medium to face-to-face meetings. When the respondents compared a telephone conference to a videoconference, the latter offered only advantages, although some costs increased. There were also some difficulties when technology failed to work as expected. Another disadvantage was the small number of users, thus limiting the potential use of videoconferencing. This last aspect is related to the critical mass discussion in Markus (1990).

Videoconferencing is a less personal medium than face-to-face meetings. It does not directly support new contacts or relationships. One respondent said: 'The small talk is important for social interaction and for creating good relations—it is a disadvantage to remove this.' Some respondents also said that it was difficult to verbalise points of view when discussing complicated matters in videoconferences. These comments are in line with MRT. It indicates that a videoconference medium is not as rich as a face-to-face meeting.

Videoconferencing is a good medium if the participants have met previously and know each other. Respondents assert that having met face-to-face, opportunities for efficient conferences and a pleasant atmosphere are created. This result is in line with Åbom (1997). The results indicate that videoconferences do not replace face-to-face meetings, as implied by the 'save travel' argument.

We have argued that face-to-face meetings are necessary for creating a relationship. The disadvantages of videoconferences become apparent mostly in comparisons with face-to-face meetings. Thus videoconferences complement personal meetings and replace telephone conferences. This can also explain the existence of a high number of multipoint videoconferences.

Hypothesis 5: The videoconference is a complement to the face-to-face meeting and can replace the telephone conference

Implementing videoconferences

Our results indicate that videoconferences have many advantages over equally rich media. However, they are still used on a limited basis and we have searched for the barriers that explain this. The main answer we have found is the limited availability of the required equipment. This is true both for the companies we interviewed and for those with whom the interviewees wanted to communicate. Another factor is the respondents' lack of familiarity with this medium. In many cases videoconferencing is installed only on a limited basis and can seldom compete seriously with other media, such as face-to-face meetings or telephone conferences. These answers are in line with the critical mass theory.

Other barriers to using videoconferencing include the need for special studios where the equipment is kept. Thus it is often more complicated to use the videoconference medium than that of the telephone conference, as the latter can often be held in one's own office. The booking routines can also give potential participants a feeling that the procedure is a complicated one. In Hård and Jamison's (1996) terminology, the old structure or routine does not support the new techniques. The videoconference changes old structures and ways of doing things, and this produces barriers to the growth of videoconferencing.

Finally, many employees still regard this medium as new. They do not feel comfortable with all of its technological details. Using videoconferences is not as efficient as it could be, since many of the advantages are not utilised.

> Hypothesis 6: The main barrier to people using the videoconference medium is its limited availability

We also tried to find how to increase the use of videoconferences by employees. One barrier is that not everyone has access to the video equipment. Another limitation is that those employees who do not travel frequently prefer travelling to face-to-face meetings instead of videoconferences, since the former allows them to get away from the office. Our respondents also claimed that the main reason for the limited use of videoconferences was that people do not have sufficient knowledge of the medium. This is true both regarding the operation of the videoconferencing, and the fact of its existence. Another argument is that introducing videoconferencing prematurely might lead to failure, since a negative attitude to the medium will continue for a long time. Overcoming these attitudes is important and can be achieved if the employees know how the system works. This factor relates to social influence. Several of the respondents emphasised that a change of attitude is necessary in order to increase the use of videoconferencing. Today, the ability to use the system is limited and this, of course, constitutes an additional barrier to an increased usage of videoconferencing.

> Hypothesis 7: The main barrier to increasing the use of videoconferencing in organisations is a negative attitude toward this medium. Sometimes this is based on earlier experiences and rumours

We have found different barriers to the use of videoconferencing, one of which is related to how familiar the users are with the medium. As we have only asked users and co-ordinators of videoconferences, we have no information about the attitudes of non-users.

Implications for the design of work, workplaces and the use of space

In this explorative study we have examined the use of videoconferencing in large Swedish companies. The study has guided us to seven hypotheses. Some of these hypotheses also have clear relevance for the design of work and workplaces and for the use of space. We can conclude that videoconferencing is definitely promising for virtual teams and other forms of collaboration, when members are located in different places. Routine meetings using videoconferencing work better if the members sometimes meet face-to-face. In these cases videoconferencing substitutes for telephone conferences. The technique makes it possible to share documents and data that the users appreciate. Today, however, videoconferencing is only a complement to face-to-face meetings. In some cases, then, videoconferencing is more time and cost efficient.

Our study also shows that it is important to have the new techniques successfully implemented. Sometimes the first implementation of videoconferencing has failed due to bad techniques or other bad experiences. This creates negative attitudes towards the medium and, in many cases, these attitudes can last for a long time within the organisation. Another barrier to a wide use of videoconferencing is its limited availability today.

It is believed, however, that in time more and more successful examples of the use of videoconferencing will become known, leading to an increase in the number of users. This implies that availability will improve and so it is possible to formulate another hypothesis.

> Hypothesis 8: In the long run videoconferencing is a technique that has to be taken into account when designing future work and workplaces. It will also give the use of space a new dimension

Conclusions

In the beginning of this chapter we raised three research questions. One asked how videoconferencing is used. The fourteen Swedish companies listed in Table 9.1 answered that. We also raised seven hypotheses in order to answer the other two questions. We found that the number of users of videoconferencing in Sweden has increased during the last 5 years, but we also saw that there are still barriers to be overcome. Probably, more user-friendly techniques and users acting as good examples are required if videoconferencing is to become more popular. We also saw that, today, videoconferencing is best suited to routine meetings, replacing telephone conferences. As this is a small explorative study, we have only been able to formulate hypotheses. We have not examined desktop systems and non-users' attitudes. Further studies, including those in other countries besides Sweden, need to be conducted in order to understand fully the use of videoconferencing and its potential.

Acknowledgement

The Swedish Transport and Communication Board (KFB) and the Swedish Foundation for Strategic Research (through IMIE) have supported this work.

Note

1 By parties we refer to communicating equipment. There can of course be several participants present at each party.

References

Åbom, C. (1997) 'Videomötesteknik i olika affärssituationer—möjligheter och hinder', Master's thesis, Department of Computer and Information Science, University of Linköping.

Arnfalk, P. (1999) *Information Technology in Pollution Prevention—Teleconferencing and Telework Used as Tools in the Reduction of Work Related Travel*, Master's thesis, International Environmental Institute, University of Lund.

Björkegren, C. and Rapp, B. (1999) 'Learning and knowledge management: a theoretical framework for learning in flexible organisations', in P.J. Jackson (ed.) *Virtual Working: social and organisational dynamics*, London: Routledge.

Campbell, J. (1997) 'The impact of videoconferenced meetings on the pattern and structure of organisational communication', *Singapore Management Review*, 19, 1: 77–95.

—— (1998) 'Participation in videoconferenced meetings: user disposition and meeting context', *Information and Management*, 34, 6: 329–38.

Carey, R. (1996) 'The future is here', *Successful Meetings*, 45, 5: 40–9.

Daft, R. and Lengel, R. (1984) 'Information richness: a new approach to managerial behavior and organization design', in L. Cummings and B. Staw (eds) *Research in Organizational Behavior*, 6: 191–223; Greenwich, Conn: JAI Press.

— (1986) 'Organizational information requirements, media richness and structural design', *Management Science*, 32, 5: 554–71.

Dennis, A. and Kinney, S. (1998) 'Testing media richness theory in the new media: the effects of cues, feedback, and task equivocality', *Information Systems Research*, 9, 3: 256–74.

Egido, C. (1990) 'Teleconferencing as a technology to support cooperative work: its possibilities and limitations', in J. Galegher, R.E. Kraut, C. Egido (eds) *Intellectual Teamwork: the social and technological bases of cooperative work*, Hillsdale, NJ: Lawrence Erlbaum Associates.

Feldman, J. (1993) 'Bane of business travel?', *Air Transport World*, 30, 9: 44–9.

Fulk, J. (1993) 'Social construction of communication technology', *Academy of Management Journal*, 36, 5: 921–50.

Fulk, J. and Boyd, B. (1991) 'Emerging theories of communication in organizations', *Journal of Management*, 17, 2: 407–46.

Fulk, J. and Steinfeld, C.W. (eds) (1990) *Organisations and Communication Technology*, Newbury Park, CA: Sage Publications, 117–40.

Huber, G. and Daft, R. (1987) 'The information environments of organizations', in F.M. Jablin, L.L. Putnam, H. Karlene, L.W. Porter (eds) *Handbook of Organizational Communication*, Newbury Park, CA: Sage Publications.

Hård, M. and Jamison, A. (1996) *Successful and Failing Challengers: diesel and steam as alternatives to the gasoline automotive engine*, Stockholm: KFB-Meddelande: 14.

Johansson, S. and Stenbacka, S. (1995) *Sett och hört via bildkommunikation—användningsområden och erfarenheter*, Stockholm: Teldok rapport 96.

Karahanna, E. and Straub, D. (1999) 'The psychological origins of perceived usefulness and ease-of-use', *Information and Management*, 35, 4: 237–50.

King, R. and Weidong, X. (1997) 'Media appropriateness: effects of experience on communication media choice', *Decision Sciences*, 28, 4: 877–910.

Kydd, C. and Ferry, D. (1994) 'Managerial use of video conferencing', *Information and Management*, 27, 6: 369–75.

Lengel, R. and Daft, R. (1988) 'The selection of communication media as an executive skill', *The Academy of Management Executive*, 2, 3: 225–32.

Lindström, J. (1996) *Chefers användning av kommunikationsteknik*, Master's thesis No. 587, Institutionen för Datavetenskap (Department of Computer and Information Science), University of Linköping.

Lindström, J. (1999) *Does Distance Matter? On Geographical Dispersion in Organisations*, Doctoral Thesis No. 567, Institutionen för Datavetenskap (Department of Computer and Information Science), University of Linköping.

Maltz, E. (2000) 'Is all communication created equal? An investigation into the effects of communication mode on perceived information quality', *The Journal of Product Innovation Management*, 17, 2: 110–27.

Markus, L. (1990) 'Toward a 'Critical Mass' theory of interactive media', in J. Fulk and C. Steinfield (eds) *Organizations and Communication Technology*, Newbury Park, CA: Sage Publications: 194–218.

Markus, L. (1994) 'Electronic mail as the medium of managerial choice', *Organization Science*, 5, 4: 502–27.

Rapp, B. (1993) 'Informationshantering på individ- och organisationsnivå', in L. Ingelstam and L. Sturesson (eds) *Brus över landet—om informationsöverflödet, kunskapen och människan*, Stockholm: Carlsson Bokförlag: 117–41.

Rapp, B. and Rapp, B. (1999) *Flexibla organisationslösningar, Om flexibla arbetsformer och flexibla kontor* (Flexible organisational solutions. About flexible forms of work and flexible offices. In Swedish), Stockholm: Telematik 2001, KFB and Teledok.

Rapp, B. and Skåmedal, J. (1996) *Telekommunikationers implikationer på resandet*, Stockholm: KFB-rapport: 2.

Rognes, R. (1999) *Telecommuting: Organisational Impact of Home-based Telecommuting*, Stockholm, Doctoral thesis, EFI, Handelshögskolan.

Schmitz, J. and Fulk, J. (1991) 'Organizational colleagues, media richness, and electronic mail', *Communication Research*, 18, 4: 487–523.

Sitkin, S.B., Sutcliffe, K.M. and Barrios-Choplin, J.R. (1992) 'A dual-capacity model of communication media choice in organizations', *Human Communication Research*, 18, 4: 563–98.

Sproull, L. and Kiesler, S. (1986) 'Reducing social context cues: electronic mail in organizational communicetion', *Management Science*, 32, 11: 1492–512.

Sturesson, L. (2000) *Distansarbete—teknik, retorik, praktik*, Doctoral thesis, Studies in Arts and Sciences, University of Linköping.

Trevino, L.K., Daft, R.L. and Lengel, R.H. (1990) 'Understanding managers' media choices: a symbolic interactionist perspective', in J. Fulk and C. Steinfield (eds) *Organizations and Communication Technology*, Newbury Park, CA: Sage Publications: 71–94.

Webster, J. (1998) 'Desktop videoconferencing: experiences of complete users, wary users, and non-users', *MIS Quarterly*, 22, 3: 257–86.

Webster, J. and Trevino, L. (1995) 'Rational and social theories as complementary explanations of communication media choices: two policy-capturing studies', *Academy of Management Journal*, 38, 6: 1544–72.

Yates, J. and Orlikowski, W. (1992) 'Genres of organizational communication: a structurational approach to studying communication and media', *The Academy of Management Review*, 17, 2: 299–326.

10 Potential research methods for studying a virtual workplace

Pertti Järvinen

Introduction

The academic field of information systems has developed because organisations use a specialised body of knowledge about information and communication systems. Teaching and research support these organisational needs; Davis (2000) has differentiated between two main approaches in the methods used: the functionalist and the interpretative. He identifies a significant variety of methods employed in information systems and, hence, holds information systems to be a more mature science than many other neighbouring sciences. This plurality of potential methods and the importance of the correct selection have been emphasised in a series of three conferences concerning methods (Mumford *et al.* 1985; Nissen *et al.* 1991; Lee *et al.* 1997).

Behind the individual research methods there are research philosophies, such as logical empiricism, critical rationalism, critical theory, phenomenology, hermeneutics and systems theory (Higgs 1995). The abstraction level of those research philosophies is rather high and they therefore offer little advice to researchers on how to perform a certain study in practice. On the other hand, Galliers and Land (1987) found at least ten traditional and newer (both quantitative and qualitative) research methods and approaches, with Tesch (1990) identifying twenty-seven qualitative research methods. The number of different methods is thus rather large; it might therefore be reasonable to limit the number of methodological categories in one way or other.

By considering research questions and research objects, Järvinen (2000) developed a taxonomy with six research approaches (Figure 10.1) for guiding researchers in finding an appropriate research approach. The number of categories in the taxonomy is so small that it does not exceed the mental capacity of the human short-term memory: 5 ± 2 observational units (von Wright 1979). Järvinen also demonstrated that his taxonomy is in many aspects better than some earlier classifications (Galliers and Land 1987; Nunamaker *et al.* 1991; March and Smith 1995).

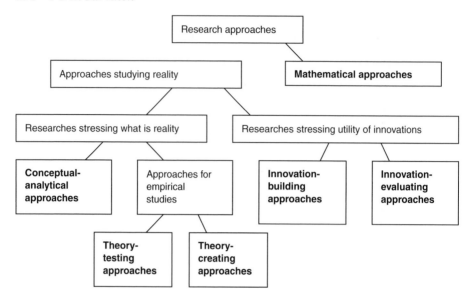

Figure 10.1 Järvinen's taxonomy of research methods

In normal circumstances, half the population of industrialised countries belongs to the workforce and, considering the normal day of an employed person and the period he or she is awake, half this period is taken up at work. In addition, work plays a central role in the development of the personal identity and to this end work-related research is important.

With the advent of computers, we now have commercially available and popular products that allow virtual environments to be built, evaluated and used from anywhere and at any level—from individual applications to worldwide networks. This new innovation will penetrate into markets and into many workplaces. Hence it would be interesting to combine Järvinen's taxonomy with the six classes of research approaches and virtual workplaces, and to test *which kind of research questions can be studied with different research approaches into virtual working places*.

We shall proceed by first presenting the taxonomy and characterising different research approaches. Thereafter we shall create one or more tentative research questions for each class of research approaches. The consequence, as we will see, is some novel findings.

Taxonomy of research objects and methods

In the development of our taxonomy, the top-down principle is applied: that is, all the research approaches are first divided into two classes; one or both are then again divided into two sub-classes (see Figure 10.1). At the beginning we differentiate other methods from mathematical methods, because they concern formal languages, algebraic units, etc., in other words, symbolic systems which have no direct reference to objects in reality. From the rest of the methods concerning reality, we then use research questions for differentiation. Two classes are based on whether the research question refers to what is a (part of) reality or whether it stresses the utility of an innovation, usually an artefact (something made by human beings). From the former we differentiate conceptual-analytical approaches (i.e. methods for theoretical development) from empirical research approaches. When the past and present are empirically studied, we differentiate the theory-testing or theory-creating methods, depending on whether there is a theory, a model or a framework guiding the study or whether a researcher is developing a new theory grounded in the gathered raw data. Regarding innovations or artefacts, we also differentiate between building and evaluating them.

To give a more concrete view of our classifications, we also enumerate the research methods involved. There are, however, some methods (for example, the case study) that have many variants belonging to more than one approach (see Cunningham 1997 and Järvinen 2000).

If, in *mathematical* studies, a certain theorem, lemma or assertion is proved to be true within a particular context of fundamental mathematical presuppositions, the research question could be as follows: Can we prove this theorem to be true?

In *conceptual-analytical* studies, normally two different approaches are identified. First, we can start from the assumptions, premises and axioms and derive the theory, model or framework. A researcher could then ask: Which kind of theory concerning a certain part of reality could be derived, if certain assumptions and premises are valid? Second, the basic assumptions behind constructs in previous empirical studies are first analysed; theories, models and frameworks used in those studies are identified, and logical reasoning to integrate them is thereafter applied. A researcher could then ask: Is there any common theory which describes and explains those phenomena?

In the *theory-testing* studies, such methods as laboratory experiments, surveys, field studies, field experiments, etc. are used. In a study where the theory-testing method is adopted, the theory, model or framework is either taken from the literature and developed or is refined for that study. The research question could then be: Do observations confirm or falsify that theory?

In the *theory-creating* approach we include the 'normal' case study (Yin 1989; Eisenhardt 1989), ethnographic method (van Maanen 1979), grounded theory (Strauss and Corbin 1990), phenomenography (Marton 1982), contextualism (Pettigrew 1985), discourse analysis, longitudinal study, phenomenological study, hermeneutics, and so on. A researcher could then ask: Which kind of construct or model could describe and explain the observations gathered? Which theory could explain 'why acts, events, structure and thoughts occur?' (Sutton and Staw 1995: 378)

In *building* a new innovation or artefact, utility aspects are sought and a particular information system (IS) development model is applied. The research question could be: Is it possible to build a certain innovation or artefact? In *evaluation* of the innovation or artefact (e.g. an information system) some criteria are used and some measurements undertaken. A researcher could ask: How effective is this artefact? *Action research* contains the following phases in the cyclical process: diagnosis, action planning, action taking, evaluating and specifying learning (Susman and Evered 1978). Hence, action research contains both building and evaluation within the same process. A researcher is then working with a client and the latter could ask: Could you help me and, together, could we solve this problematic situation?

Examples

In order for us to become familiar with the taxonomy of research approaches, I shall, in this section, demonstrate the classes of research approaches that present some potential research questions. In each class I shall take one or two examples from the literature and link them to the questions. It might be possible to use only one application domain in the examples and, in this way, create a common basis to compare different research approaches. One application domain might, however, overly restrict consideration, in other words, the one-sidedness of one application domain might give a restricted view on the complexity of virtual workplaces. I shall therefore try to confine the number of application domains whilst still demonstrating the different research problems in each area.

Mathematical approaches

Here I look at look at how Aulin (1989: 18–27) classified dynamic systems. The dynamic system can have either nilpotent or full causal recursion. The system with *nilpotent* recursion is in rest state. The initial state is called the 'rest state', and the nilpotent dynamic system has a property of coming back to its initial state after a finite number of time units. We can say that an external disturbance (or stimulus) occurring at the beginning throws the system out of its rest state to a perturbed state, after which the nilpotent causal recursion conducts the system back to the rest state. During its return journey, the system gives response to the stimulus. If the same stimulus is offered again, the system gives the same finite total response. Thus it is a memoryless system that does not learn from experience.

A dynamic system, with a full causal recursion, does not have any rest state to be reached in a finite number of steps (in a finite time). The causal systems can be classified into two categories: nilpotent systems with a constant goal function (in time) and systems with a full causal recursion have a continuous goal function in time.

The causal systems with full causal recursion can be divided into four classes depending on whether the system will *disintegrate* after a certain disturbance, with its trajectory disassociating itself from the path of its original goal function, or whether the system is *steerable from outside*, with its path proceeding at a constant distance from the path of its original goal function or coming closer to the path of its original goal function in time. The latter can be either finite (*self-regulating systems*) or infinite (*self-steering systems*).

In order to obtain definite views on the classes above we shall show which real system belongs to each category. If the uniqueness of the states of mind, along with the goal-oriented nature of thought processes, is typical of human consciousness, the only thinkable causal representation of what takes place in the human mind in an alert state is the self-steering process. According to Aulin (1989: 173) it is, however, necessary to limit this interpretation so that what is termed 'self-steering' in the human mind is the *total* intellectual process. None of the partial processes need be self-steering.

Real-world examples of self-regulating systems are: a ball in a cup that has the form of a half-sphere, a room equipped with a good thermostat, some living organisms like the heart, etc. A flying ball (the resistance of the air is negligible), a frictionless oscillator and a robot are examples of systems steerable from outside. A radioactive atom and a dead organism are disintegrating systems.

Mowshowitz (1997) characterised *virtual organisation* in terms of four basic management activities that depend on separating requirements from satisfiers:

I.   Formulation of abstract requirements (e.g. requests for information);
II. Tracking and analysis of concrete satisfiers (e.g. information services);
III. Dynamic assignment of concrete satisfiers to abstract requirements on the basis of explicit criteria; and
IV. Exploration and analysis of the assignment criteria (associated with the goals and objectives of the organisation).

Mowshowitz himself related the first three features (I–III) of his virtual organisation construct to disparate phenomena, including virtual memory, network switching, virtual teams and virtual reality, by demonstrating abstract requirements, satisfiers and criteria. Mowshowitz considered these phenomena similar, but he then almost ignored the fourth feature (IV), the goal function. This observation triggers the question:

> 1.1 Do virtual memory, network switching, virtual teams and virtual reality have a similar goal function, and if not, to which ones of the Aulin's classes might each phenomenon belong?
>
> Aulin's classes are based on differences of goal function in a certain class. The pre-programmed virtual memory may have a constant goal function, but a virtual team continuously changes its goal function.

Turoff (1997) found that 'until the introduction of computers, mathematics was the only field of science in which one could invent systems with no necessary correspondence to the real world. Now, with computers, we can build virtual systems that need not correspond with the real world'. I therefore formulate the following research question:

> 1.2 Is it possible to find a new sub-category of dynamic systems by using the idea of virtuality?
>
> Aulin's classification of dynamic systems at the highest level is exhaustive, i.e. it covers all the types of dynamic systems. But there can be potential subcategories not yet found. A researcher can follow Aulin's idea to weaken one or more mathematical presuppositions and then, with mathematical analysis, derive the properties of the 'new possible world'.

Innovation-building approaches

The main line of innovation building concerns how to build a new innovation. The building covers the whole process, from the beginning to the end. This process is normally guided by a particular normative method which stipulates what should be done and when. Building those normative methods also belongs to this category. I begin by discussing the method intended for virtual software configuration management (Rahikkala 2000) and follow by considering the building as an artefact.

Rahikkala (2000: 26) defined virtual corporations as temporary, dynamically changing networks of companies, whose employees are dispersed throughout an interconnected world of information systems. A virtual software corporation is a collaboration of a number of distributed teams whose members are drawn from different companies bound together by a common goal wherein software products are developed dynamically, and which adapts itself to the customers' changing requirements by switching resources as needed (Rahikkala *et al.* 1998b). Software configuration management is a discipline for establishing and maintaining the integrity of the product of a software project throughout the project's lifecycle. Rahikkala's method for virtual software configuration management is based on the Pr^2imer framework (*Practical Process Improvement for Embedded Real*-Time Software) (Karjalainen *et al.* 1996), developed by Rahikkala *et al.* (1998a) and finalised by Rahikkala in her dissertation (2000). Her main idea for building a new method was to take some known method (Pr^2imer), intended for single-site software production, and to enlarge it by combining some new features caused by a virtual corporation. Rahikkala found the following virtual features: infrastructure, facility, security, culture, communication and switching.

Rahikkala's *method* has some clear advantages as it, or Pr^2imer, contains a component that encourages continual improvement. I, however, pose the question:

2.1 What deficiencies does Rahikkala's method have, and if found, how can it be improved?

Rahikkala conducted no competition between the previously known methods. Such a competition might have produced some better methods than Pr^2imer. I do not know of any study that has made a comparison between dynamic, flexible, and modifiable methods, such as Pr^2imer, and the constant methods; are the former better than the latter and under which circumstances? Virtual features may change in the course of time, or their importance might change. In an ideal case, the new method is proved to be better than the best one thus far. Rahikkala implicitly presented many criteria such as cost-efficiency, project management, efficiency, effectiveness etc. She did not use these criteria to prove that her results were better than the others.

The starting point for innovation, or to build an artefact, can be that a particular interested party has considered the initial state to be problematic. The same party can also have an idea to apply or to use some resources (technological, human, data/information/knowledge, financial resources) in a new way in order to solve a problem. In considering construction or a *building* task, the target state can be known or unknown. If it is known, the task of researchers as builders is to try to implement the desired change from the initial state to the target one. If the target state is unknown, we have at least two alternatives. We can first specify the target state and then try to implement measures to achieve that state, or we can realise both target-seeking and implementation in parallel. The good intentions of builders will not always materialise and the final state may differ from the target state (Figure 10.2).

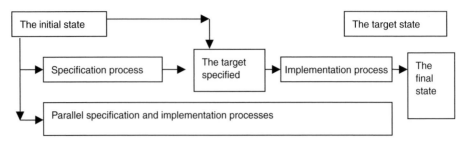

Figure 10.2 Different alternatives concerning the building process and its outcomes

March and Smith (1995) connect two models to two states, the first one to the initial state and the second one to the target state, in such a way that the models represent situations as problem and solution statements: how things are at the beginning and how they ought to be at the target state (a normative model). The (descriptive) model of the initial state may need to capture the structure of reality in order to be a useful representation. To emphasise the utility aspect motivating construction, the (problematic) initial state is evaluated by using certain utility metrics (or many), with the target state estimated to be better, more valuable, more desired with the same metrics. The model of the initial and/or target state can (but need not) contain one or more new constructs. According to March and Smith, methods are based on a set of underlying constructs (language) and a representation (model) of the solution space. Methods are often used to translate from one model or representation to another in the course of solving a problem.

By using virtual software configuration context I define the research question:

2.2 How can a virtual meeting room be built for maximising mutual understanding between teams in the virtual software corporation?

The teams located in different places and working in the same software development project must negotiate how to distribute tasks between them and decide what are the functions of different software components. The specification of the target state appears to be difficult, and I therefore guess that the required virtual meeting room will be built by carrying parallel specification and implementation processes. The main concept or idea will be similar to the video telephone studied by Kraut *et al.* (1998) in a natural experiment. In order to create the feeling of the room, the system can exploit the ideas presented in Nunamaker *et al.* (1995).

Innovation-evaluating approaches

March and Smith (1995) describe how:

> . . . research in the evaluated activity develops metrics and compares the performance of constructs, models, methods, and instantiations for specific tasks. Metrics define what a research area is trying to accomplish. Since 'the second' or subsequent constructs, models, methods, or instantiations for a given task must provide significant performance improvement, evaluation is the key activity for assessing such research.
>
> (March and Smith 1995: 261)

We shall continue with the same tentative example as above, and pose the question:

3.1 How good is the virtual meeting room in maximising mutual understanding?

  We have only one metric (mutual understanding) that is difficult to measure. Flood and Romm (1996: 64–70) presented three approaches:

a 'Design management' is intended to *co-ordinate by design*. There are two extremes: 'no structure' and 'superstructure'. In 'no structure', there is control by inefficiency and its demands. In 'superstructure', rules and procedures of the system become the controlling force.

b 'Debate management' is characterised by the expression: 'intersubjective decision making highlights the (facilitative) power of the *intersubjective process to aid decision making*'. The authors also write that power is seen as something to be used in the course of interaction. There are two extremes: 'no decisions' and 'superdecisions'. With 'no decisions', the debating process is presented to participants as if no point of decision is possible. All viewpoints are equally relevant and so there is no basis for making a choice. Here, in effect, no decisions are taken and existing power (perhaps power built into structures) prevails by default and implements its attendant biases. With 'superdecisions', ossified meanings may fix the framework within which all decisions are made.

c 'Might-right' management deals with disempowering social practices that can lead to a lack of relevance of designs, concerning (1) those who have to live with the experienced consequences of them or a lack of influence in debating processes, and (2) leaving decisions (which are ill considered) for those who have to live with and experience the consequences of them—to minimise the abuse of power (a core concern of Flood and Romm's book).

To my mind, debate management best corresponds to the main goal of the virtual meeting room. The might-right management can be used to co-ordinate the process. Flood and Romm (1996) found, between two extremes, consensus and conflict, two intermediate degrees, understanding and tolerating. Those four classes (consensus, understanding, tolerating and conflict) can be used as the first tentative trial of metric.

Conceptual-analytical approaches

I shall consider here the notion of work, especially its theoretical analysis. I will use the developmental work research (DWR) model (Engestroem 1987; Virkkunen and Kuutti 2000) as a starting point. This is based on cultural historical activity theory. There are various introductions to the DWR model but I will follow Kuutti's (1991) selection. He first considered work as a rela-tionship between two main components, i.e. between the subject and object of the activity, with emphasis placed on the mediation between the two. That basic relation is mediated by a tool (Figure 10.3).

This simple structure is not, however, adequate to fulfil the needs of a consideration of the systemic relations between an individual and his/her environment, and thus Engestroem adds a third main component, namely 'community' (those who share the same object of activity). Two new relation-ships are formed here: subject-community and community-object. Both of them need a mediating relation, too, and hence the basic structure of an activ-ity is obtained (Figure 10.4).

By referring to the basic structure of an activity and to our idea of studying the virtual workplace, I can propose many research questions:

4.1 How might a virtual workplace change the main components (subject, object and community) of an activity?

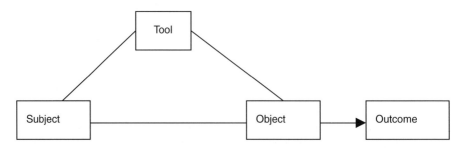

Figure 10.3 The simple model of work

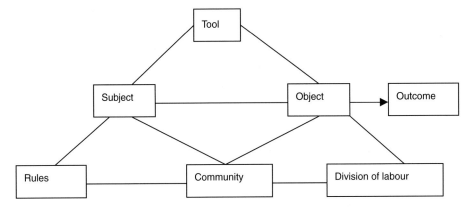

Figure 10.4 The basic structure of an activity

The subject and the object cannot be all virtual although the community can, and a researcher should model the virtual community or team (Mowshowitz 1997) by working with the subject and manipulating the object in order to produce the desired outcome.

4.2 How might a virtual workplace change the mediating relations (tool, rules and division of labour) of the activity?

The tool can contain virtual technology, and the rules that specify acceptable interactions between members of the community and the division of labour (i.e. the continuously negotiated distribution of tasks) might utilise some kind of virtuality (Turoff 1997).

4.3 What components are lacking in the basic structure of an activity and how might a virtual workplace change the current and new components?

The title refers to a workplace. This means that the community as the social environment is not the only environment, but we also have physical and informational environments. One of the better known aspects of virtuality is the new type of environment created by virtual technology. By taking the resource view we can say that the basic structure of an activity contains a division of human resources but not a division nor a distribution of either physical or informational (data, information and knowledge) resources. These observations underline the importance of question 4.3.

All these questions (4.1–4.3) can be approached from a deductive or inductive 'direction', in other words, by using certain axioms or earlier studies as a starting point, respectively.

Theory-testing approaches

Let us tentatively assume that the basic structure of an activity (Figure 10.4) won our competition, and that this theory best describes the programming activity in a virtual software corporation. Our research question could then be:

5.1 Does the basic structure of an activity describe the programming activity in a virtual software corporation?

From Figure 10.4 we can derive the variables and hypotheses, normally one hypothesis per edge in the research model (here Figure 10.4). We then select or develop a measurement instrument for every variable. Thereafter we design the research setting and select the research method. Because the controlled experiments and surveys are difficult to arrange, we select the theory-testing case method (see Lee 1989; Markus 1983). The selected case can either confirm our theory or falsify it.

Theory-creating approaches

We can assume that we do not know very much about the programming activity in a virtual software corporation, that is, there is no tentative or preliminary theory describing that activity. To this end we want to conceptualise the programming activity by studying it with different sensitive methods. We could have the following research questions:

6.1 What does the programming work mean to you?

A researcher can go and interview programming teams in a particular virtual software corporation. The interviews are normally audio taped and transcribed word-by-word. The researcher analyses the transcripts and can find different conceptions on the programming activity. Sandberg (2000) used phenomenography (Marton 1982), analysed his transcripts and found three different conceptions. In general, the result of the phenomenographical study is a variation of different conceptions. The goal of the researcher is not to find the most relevant conception: the variation, in itself, is of interest.

6.2 Which kind of programming work do you undertake in a virtual software corporation?

A researcher can interview or send a questionnaire with open questions to teams in a particular virtual software corporation. He or she then analyses the textual material received and can apply grounded theory (Strauss and Corbin 1990) with its open, axial and selective coding and produce a story. The latter tentatively describes programming work in a virtual software corporation; in other words, it is a preliminary theory, sometimes called an 'espoused theory'.

6.3 Which kind of work is programming work in a virtual software corporation?

A researcher can go to a virtual software corporation as an ethnographer (van Maanen 1979) and stay there for a long time. He or she will make both field notes and 'head notes', hold discussions with programmers, observe their work and collect data from various sources. His or her purpose is to understand the nature of programming in a virtual software corporation. After becoming native, normally after several months staying in the corporation, he or she tries to describe conceptually the programming work, which can thus be called a 'theory-in-use'. Argyris and Schön (1978) found that a researcher can see what people are doing as well as noting what they say they are doing—that is, both the theory-in-use and the espoused theory.

The latter finding, based on questions 6.2 and 6.3, and together with question 6.1, show that theory-creating research methods sometimes have few differences. Tesch (1990) found twenty-seven different research methods belonging to this category. Fortunately he suggested a 'search tree' indicating how one might find a suitable method for a certain type of research problem.

Discussion

Our examples show that virtual workplaces are a versatile research area. They also demonstrate that different research approaches are relevant to different research questions. In order to help the researcher find a suitable research approach, we have collected our results into Table 10.1. We have used the same order as above and have generalised somewhat for better applicability.

We would still like to stress that the innovation-building research approaches deviate from the traditional ones, in that they create a new reality; the innovation-evaluating research approaches differ from the traditional ones, in that they do not describe the structure and action of the new innovation but use one or more utility criteria for measuring the innovation. The connection between virtual systems and mathematical manipulations seems to open a promising avenue for further research. Regarding the activity theory, we have been somewhat critical and, hence, it needs to be further developed.

Sambamurthy and Zmud (2000) considered the information technology (IT) imperatives within the digital economy and the conceptualisation of the organising logic for IT activities. In the latter they recommended thinking about the organisation of IT activities, first and foremost, as the establishment of a

Table 10.1 Research approaches and research questions

Research approaches	Exemplary research questions (generalised)
1. Mathematical	To which system class will this subsystem belong? Does a certain aspect, e.g. virtuality, cause changes in the classification of dynamic systems, and which kind of properties can be proved to exist in that class?
2. Innovation-building	Could we improve a certain method? Can we build a certain innovation with specific goals?
3. Innovation-evaluating	How good is a certain innovation measured by particular criteria?
4. Conceptual-analytical	How will a certain new aspect change components or relations in a particular theory, model or framework? Are some components or relations lacking or useless in a particular theory, model or framework?
5. Theory-testing	Do observations confirm or falsify a particular theory, model or framework?
6. Theory-creating	What does a certain action mean for you? Which kind of action is yours? Which kind is a certain action?

platform that provides a rich ensemble of current and future IT-enabled functionalities (see Ciborra 1996). They wrote that the platform organising logic is composed of three essential building blocks: IT capabilities, relational structures, and integration architectures. In his Olivetti case study, Ciborra (1996) found that the successive technology life cycles are longer than the product life cycles. Therefore a firm's formal structure changes very frequently and abruptly, while the informal networks remain relatively stable. Hence the platform organisation cannot be identified with the formal structure: it is a much more elusive bedrock, harder to recognise and analyse as an organisational arrangement. Ciborra (1996) summarised his paper by stating that the platform is far from being a specific organisational structure, where one can recognise a new configuration of authority and communication lines. The platform is based on a community, a pool of human resources, which can be described in the Olivetti case as the old boys' network at top management level.

The discussion above clearly demonstrates that we shall have an increasing number of job and work redesign issues in the future. This suggests a need for self-evaluation and outside-evaluation of work and workplaces, both in IT and other industries. New technological, organisational and informational innovations at work will then be necessary and more innovation-building and evaluating studies will be needed.

We have shown that subjectivist and objectivist theories are restricted, and we therefore need theories based on the subject–object interaction, supplemented by its context. If we want to analyse the consequences of the real/virtual pairing, we can say that both the object and context can be real or virtual. If the subject is individual, she or he must be real, but if the subject is a team, some members can be virtual. Because we only have a few studies on the virtual aspect of work, we must, in future, focus our theoretical attention to virtual aspects of work and, as we recommend, we must then reconsider every element of the triplet: subject, object and context.

Some aspects of virtuality can only be studied indirectly, and then mathematical approaches are necessary. Some aspects are based on experiences, and then, particularly, exploratory theory-creating studies are needed. Some findings can later be confirmed with theory-testing studies. We can conclude that the virtual aspect at work creates so many different research questions that all the research approaches in Figure 10.1 and Table 10.1 are necessary.

Acknowledgement

I am especially thankful to the editors for their constructive comments on the earlier versions of this chapter.

References

Argyris, C. and Schön, D. (1978) *Organizational Learning: a theory of action perspective*, Reading Mass: Addison-Wesley.

Aulin, A.Y. (1989) *Foundations of Mathematical System Dynamics: the fundamental theory of causal recursion and its application to social science and economics*, Oxford: Pergamon Press.

Ciborra, C.U. (1996) 'The platform organization: recombining strategies, structures, and surprises', *Organization Science*, 7, 2: 103–18.

Cunningham, J.B. (1997) 'Case study principles for different types of cases', *Quality and Quantity*, 31, 4: 401–23.

Davis, G.B. (2000) 'Information systems conceptual foundations: looking backward and forward', in R. Baskerville, J. Stage and J. DeGross (eds) *Organizational and Social Perspectives on Information Technology*, Boston: Kluwer.

Eisenhardt, K.M. (1989) 'Building theories from case study research', *Academy of Management Review*, 14, 4: 532–50.

Engestroem, Y. (1987) *Learning by Expanding: an activity theoretical approach to developmental research*, Helsinki: Orienta-konsultit.

Flood, R.L. and Romm, N.R.A. (1996) *Diversity Management: triple loop learning*, Chichester: Wiley.

Galliers, R.D. and Land, F.F. (1987) 'Choosing appropriate information systems research methodologies', *Communications of ACM*, 30, 11: 900–2.

Higgs, P.H. (1995) 'Metatheories in philosophy of education: introductory overview', in P.H. Higgs (ed.) *Metatheories in Philosophy of Education*, Johannesburg: Heinemann.

Järvinen, P. (2000) 'Research questions guiding selection of an appropriate research method', in H.R. Hansen, M. Bichler and H. Mahrer (eds) *Proceedings of ECIS2000*, 3–5 July, Vienna University of Economics and Business Administration.

Kraut, R.E., Rice, R.E., Cool, C. and Fish, R.S. (1998) 'Varieties of social influence: the role of utility and norms in the success of a new communication medium', *Organization Science*, 9, 4: 437–53.

Kuutti, K. (1991) 'Activity theory and its applications to information systems research and development', in H.-E. Nissen, H. Klein and R. Hirschheim (eds) *Information Systems Research: contemporary approaches and emergent traditions*, Amsterdam: Elsevier.

Lee, A.S. (1989) 'A scientific methodology for MIS case studies', *MIS Quarterly*, 13, 1: 33–50.

Lee, A., Liebenau, J. and DeGross, J. (eds) (1997) *Information Systems and Qualitative Research*, London: Chapman and Hall.

March, S.T. and Smith, G.F. (1995) 'Design and natural science research on information technology', *Decision Support Systems*, 15: 251–66.

Markus, M.L. (1983) 'Power, politics, and MIS implementation', *Communications of ACM*, 26, 6: 430–44.

Marton, F. (1982) *Towards Phenomenography of Learning: I. Integratial experiential aspects*, Gothenburg: University of Gothenburg, Dept. of Education, 6.

Mowshowitz, A. (1997) 'Virtual organization', *Communications of ACM*, 40, 9: 30–7.

Mumford, E., Hirschheim, R., Fitzgerald, G. and Wood-Harper, A.T. (eds) (1985) *Research Methods in Information Systems*, Amsterdam: North-Holland.

Nunamaker, J.F., Chen, M. and Purdin, T.D.M. (1991) 'Systems development in information systems research', *Journal of Management Information Systems*, 7, 3: 89–106.

Nunamaker, J.F., Briggs, R.O. and Mittleman, D.D. (1995) 'Electronic meeting systems: ten years of lessons learned', in D. Coleman and R. Khanna (eds) *Groupware: Technologies and Applications*, Upper Saddle River: Prentice Hall, 149–93.

Pettigrew, A.M. (1985) 'Contextualist research and the study of organisational change processes', in E. Mumford, R. Hirschheim, G. Fitzgerald and A.T. Wood-Harper (eds) *Research Methods in Information Systems*, Amsterdam: North-Holland.

Rahikkala, T. (2000) *Towards virtual software configuration management: a case study*, Espoo: VTT—Technical Research Centre of Finland.

Rahikkala, T., Taramaa, J. and Vaelimaeki, A. (1998a) Industrial experiences from SCM current state analysis, in B. Magnusson (ed.) *System Configuration, System Configuration Management*, ECOOP 98, Berlin: Springer-Verlag.

Rahikkala, T., Blackwood, R., Cocchio, L., Gray, E., Kucza, T., Newman, J. and Vaelimaeki, A. (1998b) 'Experiences from requirement analysis for SCM process improvement in virtual software corporations', in *Proceedings of European Conference on Software Process Improvement SPI '98*.

Sambamurthy, V. and Zmud, R.W. (2000) 'Research commentary: the organizing logic for an enterprise's IT activities in the digital era—a prognosis of practice and a call for research', *Information Systems Research*, 11, 2: 105–14.

Sandberg, J. (2000) 'Understanding human competence at work: an interpretive approach', *Academy of Management Journal*, 43, 1: 9–25.

Strauss, A. and Corbin, J. (1990) *Basics of qualitative research: grounded theory procedures and techniques*, Newbury Park: Sage Publications.

Susman, G.I. and Evered, R.D. (1978) 'An assessment of the scientific merits of action research', *Administrative Science Quarterly*, 23, 582–603.

Sutton, R.I. and Staw, B.M. (1995) 'What theory is not', *Administrative Science Quarterly*, 40, 3: 371–84.

Tesch, R. (1990) *Qualitative Research: analysis types and software tools*, New York: Falmer.

Turoff, M. (1997) 'Virtuality', *Communications of ACM*, 40, 9: 38–43.

Van Maanen, J. (1979) 'The fact of fiction in organizational ethnography', *Administrative Science Quarterly*, 24, 539–50.

Virkkunen, J. and Kuutti, K. (2000) 'Understanding organizational learning by focusing on "activity systems"', *Accounting, Management & Information Technology*, 10, 4: 291–319.

von Wright, J. (1979) 'On the limitations of human information processing' (Ihmisen tiedonka-sittelykyvyn rajoituksia, in Finnish), *Academia Scientiarum Fennica, Vuosikirja—Year Book 1979*, 163–71.

Yin, R.K. (1989) *Case Study Research: design and methods*, Beverly Hills: Sage Publications.

Index